Stevenson College Edinburgh.
Library

A20341

LIBRARY 914-42 WIL

WITHDRAWN A20344 A20341

Bertrams	08.07.05
22.7 05 AL	£5.99
7/05 BT	

Normandy

by Nia Williams

Nia Williams is a freelance writer. She has
written about travel and history for several
guides to Britain (particularly Wales) and
France, as well as contributing features to
magazines and radio.

Above: *enticing window display in a Normandy
boulangerie*

Stevenson College Edinburgh
Bankhead Ave EDIN EH11 4DE
AA Publishing

A coffee and time to let the world go by – part of the Norman experience

Written by Nia Williams
Updated by Laurence Phillips

Published and distributed in the United Kingdom by AA Publishing, a trading name of Automobile Association Developments Limited, whose registered office is Southwood East, Apollo Rise, Farnborough, Hampshire, GU14 0JW. Registered number 1878835.

© Automobile Association Developments Limited 1999, 2001, 2005
Maps © Automobile Association Developments Limited 1999 2001, 2005
This edition 2005. Information verified and updated.

Automobile Association Developments Limited retains the copyright in the original edition © 1999 and in all subsequent editions, reprints and amendments.

A CIP catalogue record for this book is available from the British Library.

All rights reserved. No part of this publication may be reproduced, stored in a retrieval system, or transmitted in any form or by any means – electronic, photocopying, recording or otherwise – unless the written permission of the publishers has been obtained beforehand. This book may not be sold, resold, hired out or otherwise disposed of by way of trade in any form of binding or cover other than that in which it is published, without the prior consent of the publisher.

The contents of this publication are believed correct at the time of printing. Nevertheless, the publishers cannot be held responsible for any errors or omissions or for changes in the details given in this guide or for the consequences of any reliance on the information provided by the same. This does not affect your statutory rights. Assessments of attractions, hotels' restaurants and so forth are based upon the author's own experience and, therefore, descriptions given in this guide necessarily contain an element of subjective opinion which may not reflect the publisher's opinion or dictate a reader's own experience on another occasion.

We have tried to ensure accuracy in this guide, but things do change and we would be grateful if readers would advise us of any inaccuracies they may encounter.

Find out more about AA Publishing and the wide range of travel publications and services the AA provides by visiting our website at www.theAA.com/bookshop

A01990

Colour separation: Keenes, Andover, Hampshire
Printed and bound in Italy by Printers Trento S.r.l.

Contents

About this Book

KEY TO SYMBOLS

➕ map reference to the maps found in the What to See section (see below)

✉ address or location

☎ telephone number

🕐 opening times

🍴 restaurant or café on premises or near by

🚇 Rouen Métrobus

🚌 nearest bus/tram route

🚉 nearest overground train station

⛴ ferry crossings and boat excursions

ℹ tourist information

♿ facilities for visitors with disabilities

✋ admission charge

↔ other places of interest near by

❓ other practical information

➤ indicates the page where you will find a fuller description

✈ travel by air

This book is divided into five sections to cover the most important aspects of your visit to Normandy.

Viewing Normandy pages 5–14
An introduction to Normandy by the author
  Normandy's Features
  Essence of Normandy
  The Shaping of Normandy
  Peace and Quiet
  Normandy's Famous

Top Ten pages 15–26
The author's choice of the Top Ten places to see in Normandy, listed in alphabetical order, each with practical information.

What to See pages 27–90
The three main areas of Normandy, each with its own brief introduction and an alphabetical listing of the main attractions
  Practical information
  Snippets of 'Did you know…' information
  2 suggested walks
  4 suggested tours
  2 features

Where To... pages 91–116
Detailed listings of the best places to eat, stay, shop, take the children and be entertained.

Practical Matters pages 117–24
A highly visual section containing essential travel information.

Maps
All map references are to the individual maps found in the What to See section of this guide.
For example, Dieppe has the reference ➕ 29E4 – indicating the page on which the map is located and the grid square in which the town is to be found. A list of the maps that have been used in this travel guide can be found in the index.

Prices
Where appropriate, an indication of the cost of an establishment is given by € signs:
€€€ denotes higher prices, €€ denotes medium prices, while € denotes lower charges.

Star Ratings
Most of the places described in this book have been given a separate rating:

✪✪✪   Do not miss
✪✪   Highly recommended
✪   Worth seeing

4

Viewing Normandy

Above and right: *two
Norman delights – apples on
the bough and music in the
streets*

Nia Williams's Normandy

Hearth and Home
Timber-framed houses and barns are found all over central and northeast Normandy. The frames, fitted together on the ground and hoisted into place, have either an infill of clay, straw and manure, or the added strength and decoration of brick. In central and west Normandy golden Caen stone gives town buildings a mellow glow, and on the sea-battered northwestern coast dark granite is used to withstand the elements.

Normandy is a region that denies any simple description. Its long coastline takes in family resorts, lonely windswept dunes and rocky cliffs, while inland there are marshlands, deep river gorges and gentle farmland. Indeed, the whole region is composed of natural 'territories', such as the Pays d'Auge, the Perche and the Suisse Normande.

Time often seems to have frozen in the villages and ancient woodlands – but my own fascination is with the history that survives in the Normandy landscape. To me, the crumbling abbey ruins tell a turbulent story of religious fervour, scholarly debate and revolutionary destruction. A solid donjon, an elegant château or a market town's startlingly elaborate parish church all speak of the changing fortunes of a once formidable political power. And I am equally drawn to the many towns that have recovered and reinvented themselves after wartime devastation; after all, the concrete and glass town that replaced Le Havre's shattered centre is as evocative in its way as are the bunkers and war museums of the D-Day beaches.

We each come in search of a different Normandy: some to see the salvaged architecture of Rouen's glorious past, or the bizarre, man-made peak of le Mont-St-Michel. Others come to remember the battles of 1944 – or simply to enjoy the delicious cider, calvados, cheese and seafood. Whatever you search for in your own Normandy, this large, varied and always surprising region is unlikely to disappoint.

Left: *the 12th-century Château Gaillard still dominates the town of les Andelys*

Normandy's Features

Geography
- 14,500km of rivers and streams. Longest river: the Seine.
- 600km of coastline.
- Highest hills: Mont des Avaloirs and the Signal d'Écouves (both 417m).
- Regional parks: Parc Naturel Régional de Brotonne (58,000ha); Parc Naturel Régional Normandie-Maine (234,000ha); Parc Naturel Régional des Marais du Cotentin et du Bessin (125,000ha).
- Regions: Haute-Normandie (upper Normandy) and Basse-Normandie (lower Normandy).
- Area: Haute-Normandie – 12,301sq km; Basse-Normandie – 17,589sq km.

Much of Normandy's landscape reflects the importance of dairy farming in its economy

Politics and Society
- Five *départements* (administrative areas): Seine-Maritime and Eure (Haute-Normandie); Manche, Orne and Calvados (Basse-Normandie).
- Population: Haute-Normandie – 1,760,000; Basse-Normandie – 1,404,000; Rouen – 380,100.
- Main regional newspaper: *Paris-Normandie*, produced at Rouen.
- Main religion: Roman Catholicism.

Transport and Industry
- Main economic activities: farming, fishing, tourism, textiles, oil refining.
- Major ferry ports: Cherbourg, Dieppe, Le Havre and Ouistreham.
- Main bridges across the Seine: Pont de Normandie (1995) – 2,141m long; Pont de Tancarville (1959) – 1,400m long; Pont de Brotonne (1977) – 1,280m long.

Say the Word
Norman place-names and family names are a mixture of Scandinavian, English and Frankish influences. The language once used by Normans has survived – just – as a patois spoken by a diminishing number on the Channel Islands. Linguists describe it as having a harder, more guttural sound than standard French, and it uses expressions derived from English and the Scandinavian languages.

Essence of Normandy

Normandy's greatest attraction is its variety, and each visit reveals new discoveries. The northeast coast offers old-fashioned seaside resorts, complete with mini-golf and fish stalls; the central Côte Fleurie is where up-market sun-worshippers display their jewellery; and in the west visitors can enjoy deserted dunes and wild rocky shores. Inland there are opportunities for hikers, canoeists and horse riders; and for lovers of architecture and history there's no shortage of medieval abbeys, beautiful churches, ruined castles and formidable châteaux. The only problem is deciding where the essence of Normandy lies for you.

THE 10 ESSENTIALS

*If you only have a short time to visit Normandy,
or would like to get a really complete picture of
the region, here are the essentials:*

• **Climb to the top** of le Mont-St-Michel (► 24–25) – it's a long haul, but well worth it for the outstanding views of the bay and the mount itself, casting its distinctive shadow across the sands.

• **Stroll through the beech woods** – the Forêt de Lyons, for example (► 43) – and enjoy their grace and silvery light.

• **Order a dish of fresh seafood** (*assiette de fruits de mer*) at a harbourside restaurant in Dieppe or Honfleur (► 21, 23).

• **Buy a snack** at a *pâtisserie*: there's one in nearly every town and village, and whatever you choose will be fresh and delicious.

• **Get off the beaten track** and explore the inland countryside: abbeys, châteaux and other sites are well signposted, and timber-framed farm buildings and turreted mansions can be found even along the most remote and unpromising country lanes.

• **Drive to the tip of the Cotentin peninsula (Cap de la Hague)** and look out past the lighthouse for dramatic views across the English Channel (► 82).

• **See the 'land of horses'** from horseback (► 115) – or watch the best of the breeds on parade at le Pin-au-Haras national stud (► 70).

• **Browse among the stalls** of one of the weekly markets (► 107), where you can find a rich assortment of fresh fruit and vegetables, live chickens and rabbits, home-baked cakes, antiques ...

• **Cross the Seine** by ferry at Duclair, west of Rouen, or across the bow-backed Pont de Normandie, for a sense of the meandering course of the river.

• **Get a real taste of Normandy** by trying cider with your meal, a selection of the region's cheeses (► 76–77), and a *trou normand* – a glass of calvados between courses.

*Fermented apples are used to make the popular brandy, calvados
Above: fresh fruit and vegetables on sale in a Normandy market
Left: fishing boats unload their catch at the Dieppe quayside*

The Shaping of Normandy

900 BC
Celts arrive in northeast France and settle along the Seine (the 'tin road'), trading Cornish tin.

58–1 BC
Much of Normandy becomes part of Roman 'Armorica'. Walled towns are built – *Rotomagus* (Rouen), *Mediolanum* (Évreux), *Noviomagus* (Lisieux), *Caracotinum* (Harfleur).

3rd–5th centuries AD
Christianity begins to spread. Germanic migrations.

485–500
As the Roman Empire disintegrates the Franks, led by Clovis, occupy parts of Normandy.

6th–8th centuries
Religious centres founded at St-Wandrille (649), Jumièges (654), le Mont-St-Michel (709).

800
First coastal raids by Vikings ('Northmen').

9th century
Vikings make their way along the Seine, attacking Rouen and Jumièges (841), and reach Bayeux in 858.

911
King Charles the Simple accepts the Vikings' presence, making their leader Rollo (Hrølf the Walker) the first duke of Normandy.

933
Cotentin peninsula brought into the duchy by Duke William Longsword.

1027
Birth of William the Bastard (later the Conqueror) to Duke Robert of Normandy at Falaise.

1066
Norman invasion of England. Duke William defeats Harold at Hastings and becomes king of England.

1087
William dies in Rouen and is buried in the Abbaye aux Hommes, Caen.

1204
King John of England loses Normandy to Philippe Auguste, king of France.

1315
Norman charter gives the region independent tax-raising powers.

1346
Hundred Years War between France and England begins with the invasion of Normandy by King Edward III of England.

1431
Jeanne d'Arc, reviver of French fortunes, is burned at the stake in Rouen by the English.

1450
King Charles VII of France regains Normandy.

1517
New port established at Le Havre.

1589
After years of religious war, Protestant King Henri IV of France defeats Catholics at Arques and Ivry-la-Bataille. Edict of Nantes (1598) grants limited rights to Huguenots (Protestants).

1608
Samuel de Champlain leaves Honfleur to found Québec.

1685
Revocation of the Edict of Nantes by Louis XIV. Mass emigration of Huguenots leaves the Norman textile industry in decline.

1789
The French Revolution: Caen is a stronghold of the republican Girondin faction – but much of Normandy remains royalist.

1793
Girondins lay siege to Granville and defeat its Chouan (royalist) defenders.

1806–43
Development of coastal

Left: a triumphal statue of William the Conqueror in his birthplace, Falaise

resorts, helped by the growth of railways, and ships between Dieppe and Newhaven, England.

1883–1926
Impressionist painter Claude Monet lives and works at Giverny.

1940
German occupation of Normandy.

1944
D-Day landings by British, Commonwealth and American forces; the Battle of Normandy.

1954
Election of a new president of the Republic, René Coty, native of Le Havre.

1967
La Hague nuclear processing plant opens on Cotentin peninsula.

1974–5
Brotonne and Normandie-Maine regional parks are

American troops approach the Normandy coast on 6 June 1944

created to protect nature and heritage.

1980
Greenpeace ship *Rainbow Warrior* pursues a vessel carrying nuclear waste into Cherbourg harbour.

1983–4
Two nuclear power stations opened: Flamanville and Paluel.

1994
Fiftieth anniversary of D-Day.

1998
P&O launch first fast-ferry catamaran on the Western Channel.

2004
Conciliation theme of the 60th anniversary of D-Day. Replica of the Liberty Bell installed on the beaches.

11

Peace & Quiet

There are many ways to escape the crowds in this predominantly rural region, though few offer complete silence. Peace and quiet can mean the crashing waves on a wild coastline, or the birdsong and rustling leaves of an ancient beech forest. Only the cemeteries of World War II are places of truly profound silence.

The Countryside

The classic Norman landscape is one of scattered timber-framed farmhouses, grazing cattle, orchards and meadows. The apples and pears of the Pays d'Auge, a swathe of fertile rolling country around Lisieux, produce cider and the famous calvados brandy, while the the dairy farms provide exquisite cheeses. To the west, the area along the Orne river known as the Suisse Normande is more dramatic, its craggy slopes and wooded gorges ideal for walkers and climbers. Farther west again, at the base of the Cotentin peninsula, the region resumes a gentle, pastoral character in the *bocage*, where fields are separated by deep lanes and thick hedges. In the spring these hedgerows burst into colour as a mass of wild flowers comes into bloom.

The tranquil Forêt de Perseigne, a mixed wood of beech, oak and coniferous trees

The Forests

Normandy retains vast tracts of beech, oak and pine forest. The Forêt de Brotonne, a dense woodland enclosed in a loop of the Seine, forms the focus of the 58,000ha

Parc Naturel Régional de Brotonne. In the region's deep south the Parc Naturel Régional Normandie-Maine takes in several forests, including the 14,000ha Forêt d'Écouves, where deer and roebuck roam, and the Forêt de Perseigne (► 56) east of Alençon. The pretty village of Lyons-la-Forêt (► 43) is a perfect base for exploring the Forêt de Lyons, 11,000ha of soaring beech trees (*hêtres*). All these woodlands have rambling trails and waymarked paths.

The Cotentin (Cherbourg) Peninsula

The coastline along the northwest finger of this large peninsula takes on the stark, rugged beauty that characterises the neighbouring region of Brittany. The Cap de la Hague (► 82), at the farthest tip of land, is the place for windswept walks and wide views across the fast-flowing waters of the Alderney Race towards the Channel Islands. From here the road sweeps south to follow the western side of the peninsula past the Vauville dunes that shelter sea birds, butterflies and the tiny spring dwarf pansy. Quiet resorts such as Barneville-Carteret (► 81) punctuate long, empty beaches lower down the coast. The eastern Cotentin offers a softer landscape of woods and pastures, especially along the Val de Saire, inland of Barfleur and St-Vaast-la-Hougue.

The granite cliffs of the Cotentin peninsula, Normandy's wildest stretch of coastline

The War Cemeteries

Many people come to Normandy specifically to pay tribute to the dead of World War II; others visit the cemeteries for solitude and reflection (► 71). Among the largest British cemeteries are Bayeux, Ranville (near Pegasus Bridge), Tilly-sur-Seulles (between Caen and Balleroy) and Ryes (northeast of Bayeux). American cemeteries are found at St-James (between Avranches and Fougères) and Colleville-sur-Mer, while the main German cemetery is at la Cambe, northeast of Isigny-sur-Mer.

The legacy of war. Ranks of British gravestones at Ranville

Normandy's Famous

Best of the Rest
Among other people of letters and the arts associated with Normandy are: composer Erik Satie (1866–1925), born in Honfleur; painters Jean-François Millet (1814–75), born near Cherbourg, and Fernand Léger (1881–1955), from Argentan; political philosopher Alexis de Tocqueville (1805–59), whose ancestral château is on the Cotentin peninsula; Rouen-born dramatist Pierre Corneille (1606–84); writer Guy de Maupassant (1850–93), born near Dieppe; and novelist Marcel Proust (1871–1922), who often spent his holidays in Cabourg.

A self-portrait by Claude Monet (1917), painted during his years at Giverny

William the Conqueror

The future conqueror of England (1027–87) was born in Falaise (► 65), the illegitimate son of Robert the Magnificent, Duke of Normandy. After inheriting the duchy at the age of eight, he spent later years fighting hostile relatives, Norman rebels and the king of France. In return for his help during King Edward the Confessor's exile William was allegedly promised the English throne; when Edward died in 1066 he set off with an invasion fleet to claim it, defeating his rival, King Harold, at Battle near Hastings. Reputedly strong and cruel, William was also a clever politician and a devoted husband.

Gustave Flaubert

Flaubert (1821–80) grew up at the Hôtel-Dieu in Rouen where his father was a physician (► 33). His first novel, *Madame Bovary* (1857), caused a sensation with its account of the affairs and eventual suicide of a bored, young doctor's wife. Flaubert, along with his publisher and printer, was taken to court but cleared of offending public morals. His next work, *Salammbô* (1862), depicted the brutality and exoticism of ancient Carthage, and in *L'Éducation sentimentale* (1869) he described the lives and loves of mid-19th-century Parisians.

Claude Monet

Born in Paris, Monet (1840–1926) went to school in Le Havre where, at the age of 18, he met picture-framer-turned-artist Eugène Boudin (► 22, 23). Under Boudin's influence Monet abandoned the studio to paint directly from nature, using the colour and light of the Norman coast to full effect. His *Impression: Soleil levant* (1872) provided the famous label for a contemporary group of painters who strove for atmosphere rather than realism in their work. After years of poverty Monet found success in the 1880s and moved to Giverny where he created a beautiful garden, the subject of many paintings (► 42). He experimented with light and colour, producing a series of studies of Rouen cathedral in the 1890s that showed the changing effects of sunlight.

Top Ten

Above: *colourful fishing boats at Honfleur*
Right: *William the Conqueror on campaign*

1
Abbaye de Jumièges

✚ 38B1

✉ 27km west of Rouen, on D143

Once a centre of scholarship and worship, this magnificent abbey was plundered after the French Revolution and is now a haunting ruin.

☎ 02 35 37 24 02

🕐 Mid-Apr–mid-Sep, daily 9:30–7; mid-Sep–mid-Apr, daily 9:30–1, 2:30–5:30

🍴 Auberge des Ruines (€€), place de la Mairie

🚌 30 from Rouen (change buses at Duclair)

♿ Moderate (free 1st Sunday in month Oct–Apr)

↔ Rouen (➤ 26, 31–36)

With its soaring white towers, circled by rooks, Jumièges has a strangely unsettling effect. The earliest ruins – the Église St-Pierre – date from the 10th century when the Benedictine abbey was refounded to replace the 7th-century original burned by Vikings. In 1040 work began on a second church, Notre-Dame, consecrated in the presence of Duke William the Bastard. During the following 300 years Jumièges prospered, accumulating gifts and adding new buildings.

With the Hundred Years War Jumièges entered a period of insecurity and slow decline; by 1792 there were only seven resident monks and the abbey was closed. It then passed to a series of private owners: one tried to set up a factory in it; another blew up the chancel and sold off the stone. Only in 1824 did new owners put a halt to the destruction.

Notre-Dame is the most spectacular part of the former monastic complex. Its twin western towers – once with timber spires – flank the entrance into a vast roofless nave lined with bold arcades. Beyond the transepts, where the northwest column has an intricate carving of a bird, a delicate 13th-century lancet arch marks the site of the chancel chapels. 'Charles VII's Passageway' leads to the Église St-Pierre, whose own towers have now gone except for their rectangular bases. Only the outline remains of the cloisters. Behind the abbey, a flight of curving steps leads up to the 17th-century abbot's lodgings, still intact, and a small knot-garden.

Above: the abbey's towers seen from the south

2
Les Andelys & Château Gaillard

A historic timber-framed village lies at the foot of the hill where Richard the Lionheart's castle has panoramic views over the Seine Valley.

Situated on the edge of a deep loop in the Seine, at the northern end of the Forêt des Andelys, are the two towns of les Andelys. Petit Andely grew in the shadow of King Richard's castle while Grand Andely is a busy centre with a Saturday market. The ruins of **Château Gaillard** rise from a high chalk outcrop; from a distance they are barely distinguishable from the white cliffs. Richard had the castle hastily constructed – probably between 1196 and 1198 – though it became known as his 'one-year wonder' because of the speed in which it was built.

One of the five original towers still stands, as well as part of the donjon, the later governor's lodge and the curtain walls. While these squat remains still preserve an impenetrable appearance, the château fell to the French just six years after its completion, when King Philippe Auguste's soldiers entered through the latrines.

Below Château Gaillard, Petit Andely extends along the riverside, a fine collection of stone and timber buildings with carved lintels, coloured glass and swirling iron lampholders. Galleries and restaurants line the street, leading into a peaceful cobbled square overlooked by the Église St-Sauveur. Grand Andely itself has some fine town houses, as well as the 13th- to 17th-century Église Notre-Dame. The Musée Nicolas Poussin houses paintings by the artist, and the Musée Normandie-Niémen commemorates General de Gaulle's fighter squadron.

✚ 29E3

🍴 Choice of restaurants (€—€€€)

🚌 From Évreux, marked 'les Andelys'

Château Gaillard

☎ 02 32 54 04 16

🕐 Mid-Mar–mid-Nov, Wed–Mon 9–12, 2–5

♿ None

↔ Écouis (▶ 38)

✋ Cheap

Massive walls and a broad view of the Seine were the strengths of Château Gaillard

3
Bayeux: the Tapestry

🕂 50B5

✉ Centre Guillaume le Conquérant, rue de Nesmond

☎ 02 31 51 25 50

🕐 Mid-Mar–Apr, Sep–Oct, daily 9–6:30; Nov–mid-Mar, daily 9:30–12:30, 2–6; May–Aug 9–7. Closed Jan 1, Dec 25 and 2 weeks in Jan

🍴 Choice of restaurants and cafés in town (€–€€)

♿ Good

✋ Moderate

All the colour, character and action of a good film are captured in this 70m–long tapestry, commissioned to celebrate William the Conqueror's victory at Hastings.

William's half-brother Odo, Bishop of Bayeux, decided to decorate his new cathedral with a spectacular wall-hanging – the latest thing in religious fashion – to impress pilgrims and local people coming to the church. A team of embroiderers took several years to complete the frieze in eight different-coloured wools (blues, greens, reds and mustard yellow). The result, now displayed in a former seminary, traces the Norman dispute over the English royal inheritance. It begins with the aged King Edward sending his brother-in-law Earl Harold Godwinson to Normandy to inform William (allegedly) he will be the next English king. Harold's adventures include shipwreck, capture and rescue, and a thrilling ride with William's troops against the Duke of Brittany.

Duke William and Earl Harold in discussion at the palace of Rouen

Before seeing the tapestry, visitors are led past a long but useful exhibition, which suggests that the tapestry deliberately includes flashbacks and split-screen effects for dramatic impact. An audio-visual commentary then guides you all too quickly past the genuine article. The wealth of detail deserves a much longer browse: spies listening to royal conversations; the Saxons sporting droopy moustaches; Halley's Comet shooting ominously over Harold's coronation; food and wine being loaded for the invasion fleet; and, in the final battle scenes, horses mustering, galloping and falling while, in the tapestry margins, soldiers' corpses are stripped of their armour. It's so fresh and energetic that you can almost hear the din of a battle fought over 900 years ago.

4
Caen: le Mémorial

Outstanding among Normandy's many war museums, this 'Museum for Peace' examines the events leading up to World War II and looks into an uncertain future.

Across the limestone façade of le Mémorial runs the inscription: '*La douleur m'a brisée, la fraternité m'a relevée ... de ma blessure a jailli un fleuve de liberté*' ('Grief crushed me, fraternity revived me ... from my wound there sprang a river of freedom'). Conflict and hope are the themes of this museum. Hovering over the vast entrance hall is a British Hawker Typhoon aircraft; a caption notes that its 23-year-old pilot was killed when it was shot down in 1944. This is not a museum of military hardware or cold strategy: throughout its themed 'spaces' individual experience is set against the progress of world affairs. Spaces One to Three trace events from 1918 to 1944 along a spiralling walkway that descends into near-darkness. Archive material includes letters, film, photographs and a secretly taped phone conversation between the collaborator Weygand and his delegate to the armistice talks. There are harrowing images: the hopeless faces of concentration camp victims; a 17-year-old Russian patriot about to be hanged.

Beyond the walkway, displays include personal letters and footage of hand-to-hand fighting during the German advance on Stalingrad. In spaces Four and Five documentary and fictional film recreates the 1944 invasion. Post-war conflict and diplomacy are covered in Jacques Perrin's film *Hope* in Space Six, and the final space is a gallery devoted to winners of the Nobel Peace Prize.

🕂 50C4

✉ esplanade du Général Eisenhower

☎ 02 31 06 06 44

🕐 Jul–Aug, 9–8; Sep–Jun, 9–7. Closed 25 Dec, 2 weeks in Jan. Last entry 75 mins before closing

🍴 Restaurant and café (€€)

🚌 From Tour le Roy in Caen centre

♿ Very good

👛 Expensive

A Typhoon aircraft hangs above pictures of the casualties of war in le Mémorial's foyer

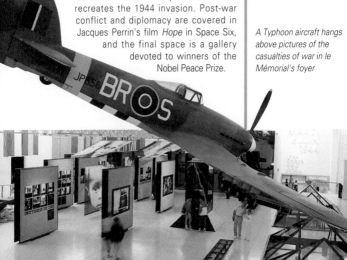

5
Château d'O

Mirrored in the waters of its moat, the towers and pointed roofs of Château d'O give it a fairy-tale charm.

✚ 51D2

☎ 02 33 35 34 69

🌐 Open selected afternoons during the summer. Telephone for details

🍴 La Ferme du Château d'O (€€–€€€) ☎ 02 33 35 36 87

🚌 From Alençon to Mortrée

♿ None

🎟 Free

↔ Argentan (▶ 55), Château de Sassy (▶ 73), Sées (▶ 74)

The château's courtyard and towers, reflected in its moat

This romantic château was built in 1484 for Jean d'O, Charles VIII's chamberlain, on the foundations of an 11th-century fortress. In 1590 a western wing was added by Jean's powerful descendant, François d'O. Having risen from governor of Caen to Henri III's superintendent of finance, François manoeuvred his way through the controversy and changing alliances of the Religious Wars, and emerged as Henri IV's counsellor. During his career he was accused of pocketing royal funds for his own use – partly to spend on this family seat.

Elaborate carvings decorate the oldest part of the château, the gatehouse, while an arcade and windows with decorative iron grilles line the 16th-century south wing. Red and black brick patterns occasionally break the pale gold and grey stone of the façade, and the O family emblem, the ermine, is carved on the south wing. A walkway leads across the moat into a three-sided courtyard, with further intricate carvings decorating the walls. Inside, the furnishings date mainly from the 18th century, and include *trompe l'œils* of Apollo and the Nine Muses, and eagles in flight, uncovered in the west wing during renovation work. The château grounds are as tranquil as the building itself: a path leads through the simple garden to woodland, and past the chapel to the orangery where exhibitions are occasionally held. Beyond the south wing, the farm buildings that once housed some of the château's household are now a restaurant.

6
Dieppe

This energetic, modern harbour town, with its delightful old quarters, offers visitors arriving by ferry a compelling first taste of France.

There's something irresistibly cheerful about Dieppe, even though it could do with a coat of paint. Once cross-Channel ferries deposited passengers opposite the quai Henri IV's hotels and restaurants, where they could then tuck into fresh seafood while watching the latest catch being unloaded on to quayside stalls. Now the ferry terminal has been shifted out of sight, yachts have moved in, and the fish stalls have been moved aside to make way for a car park. But there is still a lively pulse to the town, especially in the pedestrianised centre.

Across the water from the end of quai Henri IV the clifftop Église Notre-Dame de Bon-Secours watches over the port. The road then swings round to the shingle beach where grand old houses line the boulevard de Verdun and, in summer, snack stalls are set out along the boulevard du Maréchal Foch that runs parallel. Looming over all at the west end of the town is the 15th-century castle, whose **Musée du Château** houses a collection of carved ivory – a speciality of Dieppe in the 17th century – and paintings by Renoir, Boudin, Pissarro and Braque.

Narrow alleys lined with crumbling old houses lead from the promenade and quayside into the centre of town and to the 14th- to 16th-century Église St-Jacques, its fabric slowly being eaten away by the elements. Inside is a frieze of Brazilian natives rescued from the palace of Jean Ango, François I's naval adviser, whose fleet of priva-teers captured more than 300 Portuguese ships in the 16th century. Northeast, in the old fishing quarter, the **Cité de la Mer** has exhibitions on shipbuilding, sea life and geology.

The Grande Rue in Dieppe, always full of colour and bustle

✚ 29E4

🍴 Choice of seafood restaurants on quai Henri IV (€–€€)

🚌 From Rouen

🔁 Arques-la-Bataille (▶ 37), Château de Miromesnil (▶ 43), Varengeville (▶ 47)

Musée du Château

✉ rue Chastes

☎ 02 35 84 19 76

🕐 June–Sep daily 10–12, 2–6; Oct–May, Wed–Mon 10–12, 2–6 (Sun 6). Closed 1 Jan, 1 May, 1 Nov, 25 Dec

♿ Few

✋ Cheap

Cité de la Mer

✉ rue de l'Asile Thomas

☎ 02 35 06 93 20

🕐 Daily 10–12, 2–6 Closed 25 Dec–1 Jan

♿ Good

✋ Moderate

WITHDRAWN
Stevenson College Edinburgh
Bankhead Ave EDIN EH11 4DE

7
Le Havre: Musée des Beaux-Arts André Malraux

🕂 38A1

✉ 2 boulevard Clémenceau

☎ 02 35 19 62 62

🕓 Mon, Wed, Thu, Fri 11–6; Sat, Sun 11–7

🍴 Café (€€)

♿ Very good

✋ Cheap

↔ Honfleur (▶ 23)

This striking modern building, with its highly original walls of glass, houses an excellent display of French paintings.

Le Havre can be an oppressive place, with its endless apartment blocks and the concrete centre erected quickly after the devastation of the old town by air raids in 1944 (▶ 42). For anyone interested in Normandy's artistic heritage, though, it has the best gallery in the region.

Named after the novelist and art critic André Malraux (1901–76), the museum has undergone extensive renovation, making the most of its view over the port (through a large concrete sculpture nicknamed 'The Eye') and removing partitions inside to allow even greater light and space.

© ADAGP, Paris and DACS, London 1998

Music at the Customs House at Le Havre *by Raoul Dufy*

Malraux devised the concept of 'the museum without walls', and this building comes as near as possible to fulfilling that idea. One feature is that visitors can choose how to view the paintings: chronologically from the 17th to the 20th centuries, or beginning with the famous collection of works by Eugène Boudin (1824–98) and Raoul Dufy (1877–1953).

Boudin, who was born near by in Honfleur, represents French Impressionism along with Monet, Renoir and others. His love of painting out in the open, using free brushwork to convey the coast's huge skies and seas, earned him the title 'painter of beaches' and provided inspiration for Monet. Dufy was a native of Le Havre and one of the group of fauvist ('wild beast') painters who used bold colours to depict everyday scenes. Other artists featured include Corot, Manet, Millet and Courbet, and 17th- to 19th-century Dutch, Flemish and Italian painters.

8
Honfleur

This is one of the prettiest and most popular harbour towns in Normandy, with an old-world ambience and a distinguished maritime history.

Honfleur is about as attractive as a working port can be. Tall grey houses stand shoulder-to-shoulder along the Vieux Bassin (Old Dock), the focus of town, fishing boats cluster along the harbour near by, and shops, galleries, restaurants and hotels fill the many timber-framed and slate-fronted buildings.

The port has a long history. Its heyday as a seafaring centre was in the 17th century, when Samuel de Champlain set sail to found Québec; his achievement is noted on a plaque on the wall of the 16th-century Lieutenance, a ramshackle stone building guarding the harbour entrance, and once the home of the king's lieutenant, the governor of Honfleur. Église Ste-Catherine in the market place is remarkable for its construction by shipbuilders using wooden struts and tiles for both the main body and the 18m bell tower that stands alone across the square. The 15th-century church is dark but airy, like a great barn: two parallel naves are divided by slender timber columns and the vaulted ceiling has the look of an upturned boat. The second nave was added in 1496 to accommodate the prosperous town's growing population of sailors and ship-owners.

Not surprisingly, Honfleur was a magnet to artists in the 19th and 20th centuries. The **Musée Eugène Boudin**, named after the town's most famous son, has works by Dufy, Corot, Monet and the man himself.

✚ 38A1

🍴 Choice of restaurants and cafés (€–€€€)

🚌 From Évreux and Le Havre

↔ Le Havre (➤ 22, 42)

Musée Eugène Boudin

✉ rue de l'Homme-de-Bois, place Erik-Satie

☎ 02 31 89 54 00

🕐 Mid-Mar to Sep, Wed–Mon 10–12, 2–6; Oct–Mar, Wed–Mon 2:30–5, weekend 10–12, 2:30–5. Closed 1 Jan–10 Feb

♿ Few

✋ Moderate

Fishing boats moored in the Vieux Bassin, overlooked by distinctive, narrow dockside buildings

9
Le Mont-St-Michel

🕂 80B1

🍽 La Mère Poulard (€€), Grand Rue

🚌 From Granville and Pontorson

♿ Few; no wheelchair access to upper Mont

↔ Avranches (▶ 81)

Abbaye

☎ 02 33 89 80 00

🕐 May–Sep, daily 9–5:30; Oct–Apr, 9:30–4:30 (school hols 9:30–5)

✋ Expensive

Across its broad bay, le Mont–St–Michel rises like a vision, tapering up to the abbey spire from a chaotic pyramid of houses and shops.

In the early 8th century Bishop Aubert of Avranches had a vision in which the Archangel Michael ordered him to build a sanctuary on the isolated granite rock then known as Mont Tombe. This was no mean feat: apart from the problem of building on a sheer, narrow rock, the island is isolated by quicksands at low tide and deep water at high tide. Nevertheless, Aubert's church was finished in 708, and in the 10th century a monastery was founded on the site.

Over the centuries new buildings were added to the abbey and a town grew beneath it, clinging precariously to the steep sides. Buttresses and massive walls clamp everything fast to the rock, the church towering above the sands that have claimed the lives of many pilgrims on the last leg of their journey. Now the Mont is approached across a causeway and through the Porte du Roi. The winding Grande Rue, lined with souvenir shops and cafés, climbs towards the abbey, and steps lead off through narrow passages to the outer ramparts.

Finally, all routes lead to the **Abbaye** itself and the buildings known as 'la Merveille'. A trail passes through the refectory, cloisters and Knights' Hall, and past a huge wooden treadmill once operated by inmates when the abbey became a prison in the 18th century; the wheel was used to haul supplies straight up a

Right, top: *the Grande Rue, once crowded with medieval pilgrims, now with tourists*
Right: *le Mont, glorious in the early evening light*

24

steep ramp. Eventually steps lead down into the crypt where 10 massive columns support the abbey church. Outside, a tiny herb garden squeezed among turrets and chimneys looks out across the bay.

There are several museums on the Mont, as well as the Logis Tiphaine, home of the 14th-century military commander Bertrand du Guesclin.

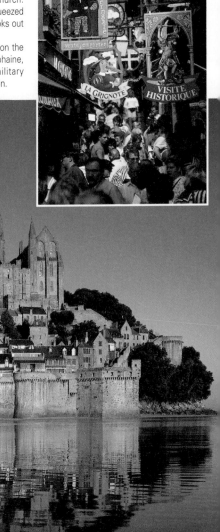

10
Rouen: rue du Gros-Horloge

✝ 34B2

🍴 Choice of restaurants and cafés, especially in and around place du Vieux-Marché (€–€€€)

🚌 From Dieppe

🚉 From Le Havre, Dieppe

↔ Rouen (➤ 31–36), Jumièges (➤ 16), Martainville (➤ 43)

🚐 Palais de Justice

🚍 8

♿ None

🖐 Cheap

❓ Ticket (panel, ➤ 33)

At the heart of Rouen's old town, this street is both a lively shopping centre and a showpiece of restored historic buildings.

There is much to admire along this pedestrianised route, where timber-framed houses have been smartly repaired, their woodwork painted in reds, pale orange and greens. The Gros-Horloge itself is an elaborate one-handed clock that sits on a stone archway spanning the street. It was originally set in the **Tour du Beffroi** (Belfry Tower) next door, but the citizens complained that it was too difficult to see; so in 1527 the arch was purpose-built and the clock moved. Despite its single hand, the Gros-Horloge manages to tell the time in hours, weeks and phases of the moon. The arch is covered in baroque carvings, including Christ the Shepherd and his flock.

The rue du Gros-Horloge links the two main focal points of old Rouen. At the west end is the place du Vieux-Marché where Jeanne d'Arc (Joan of Arc) was burned at the stake in 1431. The Église Ste-Jeanne d'Arc that marks the spot is one of Rouen's most evocative modern buildings: its wildly twisted cone of a roof extends to cover part of the central market in a design said to represent the flames that ended Joan's life. At the other end of the street is the cathedral square, dominated by the cathedral itself and surrounded by fine buildings including the city's oldest surviving Renaissance house, now the tourist office.

The Gros-Horloge, displayed for all to see on its 16th-century arch

What
to See

Above: *the intricate stonework of Rouen's cathedral*
Right: *delicate finery on show in the Alençon lace museum*

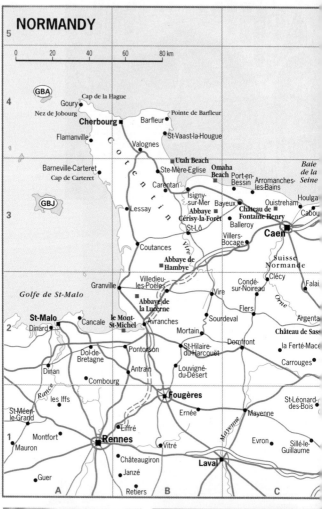

NORMANDY

0   20   40   60   80 km

(GBA)
Cap de la Hague
Goury
Nez de Jobourg
Cherbourg
Flamanville
Barfleur
Pointe de Barfleur
St-Vaast-la-Hougue
Valognes
Cotentin
Barneville-Carteret
Cap de Carteret
(GBJ)
Utah Beach
Ste-Mère-Eglise   Omaha   Baie
Beach Port-en-   de la
Bessin   Arromanches-   Seine
Carentan   les-Bains
Isigny-   Houlga
sur-Mer   Bayeux   Château de
Lessay   Abbaye   Fontaine Henry   Cabou
Cérisy-la-Forêt   Balleroy
St-Lô   Villers-   Caen
Coutances   Bocage
Vire   Suisse
Abbaye de   Normande
Hambye   Clécy
Villedieu-   Condé-   Falai
Granville   les-Poêles   sur-Noireau
Golfe de St-Malo   Abbaye de   Vire   Flers   Orne
la Lucerne   Sourdeval   Argenta
St-Malo   Cancale   le Mont-   Avranches   Château de Sass
Dinard   St-Michel   Mortain   la Ferté-Macé
Dol-de-   Pontorson   St-Hilaire-   Domfront   Carrouges
Bretagne   du-Harcouët
Dinan   Antrain   Louvigné-
Combourg   du-Désert
Rance   St-Léonard-
les Iffs   Fougères   des-Bois
St-Méen-   Ernée   Mayenne
le-Grand   Mayenne   Evron   Sillé-le-
Montfort   Liffré   Guillaume
Mauron   Rennes   Vitré   Laval
Châteaugiron
Guer   Janzé
Retiers

A   B   C

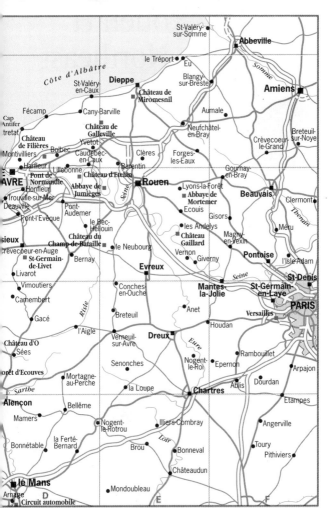

St-Valéry-sur-Somme
Abbeville
le Tréport • Eu
Blangy-sur-Breste
Amiens
Côte d'Albâtre
St-Valéry-en-Caux
Dieppe
Château de Miromesnil
Fécamp • Cany-Barville
Aumale
Cap Antifer tretat
Château de Galleville
Neufchâtel-en-Bray
Crèvecoeur-le-Grand
Breteuil-sur-Noye
Château de Filières
Bolbec Yvetot
Montivilliers
Caudebec-en-Caux
Clères
Forges-les-Eaux
Harfleur Lillebonne Barentin
Gournay-en-Bray
AVRE
Pont de Normandie
Château d'Etelan
Rouen
Lyons-la-Forêt
Beauvais
Honfleur
Abbaye de Jumièges
Abbaye de Mortemer
Clermont
Trouville-sur-Mer
Ecouis
Deauville
Pont-Audemer
le Bec-Hellouin
Gisors
Méru
Thérain
Pont-l'Evêque
Château du Champ-de-Bataille
les Andelys
Château Gaillard
Magny-en-Vexin
Pontoise
sieux
le Neubourg
Vernon
Giverny
l'Isle-Adam
rèvecoeur-en-Auge
St-Germain-de-Livet
Bernay
Evreux
St-Denis
Livarot
Conches-en-Ouche
Seine
Mantes-la-Jolie
St-Germain-en-Laye
Vimoutiers
PARIS
Camembert
Breteuil
Anet
Versailles
Gacé
Houdan
l'Aigle
Verneuil-sur-Avre
Dreux
Eure
Rambouillet
Château d'O
Sées
Senonches
Nogent-le-Roi
Epernon
Arpajon
orêt d'Ecouves
Mortagne-au-Perche
la Loupe
Chartres
Ablis
Dourdan
Sarthe
Alençon
Bellême
Etampes
Mamers
Nogent-le-Rotrou
Illiers-Combray
Angerville
Bonnétable
la Ferté-Bernard
Brou
Loir
Bonneval
Toury
Pithiviers
le Mans
Châteaudun
Arnage
Circuit automobile
Mondoubleau

Left: *evening sun over the spires and bridges of Rouen*

Far left: 'Bienvenue en Normandie ...'

Rouen &
the Northeast

Northeast Normandy stands apart from the rest of the region. This is a flat windswept country that rises to a border of white cliffs along the Côte d'Albâtre (Alabaster Coast) and the Seine Valley. Resorts and harbour towns with long seafaring histories line the seaboard – Dieppe, Le Havre, Honfleur. Inland, the Pays de Caux plateau of Seine-Maritime is dotted with aged farmhouses, churches and châteaux, while ancient beech woods gather alongside the Seine.

Farther up the river, taking in part of the Eure *département*, lies the Normandie-Vexin, a historic administrative area once bitterly fought over by the medieval kings of England and France, and guarded by strongholds such as the mighty Château Gaillard (▶ 17). There is plenty to explore here, but no trip to upper Normandy is complete without a visit to its beautiful old capital, Rouen.

' Rouen, Geneva and Pisa have been tutresses of all I know, and were mistresses of all I did, from the first moments I entered their gates. '

John Ruskin
Praeterita
(1885–9)

Rouen

Old and new Rouen oppose each other across the Seine: the new suburbs on the south bank, with their offices and tower blocks, and on the north bank a forest of Gothic spires. Venture into the old town and you encounter a fascinating world of medieval streets and busy alleyways overshadowed by the jettied gables of timber-framed houses and shops (▶ 26).

Looking along the pretty rue Damiette towards the abbey church of St-Ouen

Celts and Romans had settlements here, and a church stood on the cathedral site by AD 393. When Rollo led his Viking invaders into Normandy he chose Rouen for his capital, and by the 12th century it was being noted by a contemporary historian as a rich and pleasant town with 'great buildings, houses and churches'. A thriving weaving and textiles trade paid for more handsome buildings during the city's golden age, between the 15th and 17th centuries. After the disastrous bombardment of World War II many were painstakingly rebuilt, and today around 700 timber-framed houses survive.

But Rouen is not a city with a uniform heritage. Some streets were spared the bombing and still have a shabby, precarious look, particularly along rue St-Vivien; there you will find unpolished, lived-in corners that have changed little over the centuries. There are also striking examples of later architecture, such as the railway station. Rouen has managed to retain its character without a stifling reverence; its fine churches, museums, historic buildings and many architectural surprises are all part of a vibrant, modern city, with one of the most attractive centres in France.

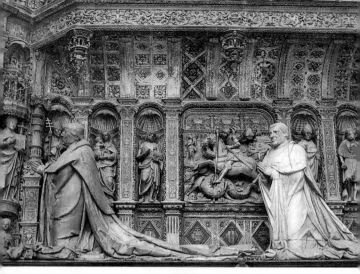

What to See in Rouen

CATHÉDRALE NOTRE-DAME　　　😊😊😊

The process of cleaning and restoring the cathedral has long obscured its intricate west façade. But gradually it is emerging from the cocoon of scaffolding, revealing its delicately worked, glittering white stone, free from the patina of years of city life.

A cathedral has stood on this site since the 4th century, though the earliest parts of the present building – apart from some 11th-century fragments – are 13th-century. Two very different towers flank the façade, giving it an eccentric yet attractive appeal. The Tour St-Romain, on the left as you face the cathedral, is crowned with a steep slate roof decorated with gold sunbursts. On the right is the ornate Tour de Beurre (Butter Tower), a 16th-century addition apparently funded by the sale of dispensations to Rouen's rich, allowing them to enjoy butter and milk during Lent. The 151m central lantern tower, L'Aigle, with its cast-iron spire, was erected in 1876, replacing a 16th-century predecessor that had burned down.

Inside, beyond the soaring nave with its two-tiered arcades, the north transept contains a glorious 14th-century rose window and, rising from the balcony, the Escalier de la Librairie (Booksellers' Stairs). Traces of Roman columns can still be seen in the crypt, and effigies of Rollo, his son William Longsword, Henry, son of Henry II of England, and Richard the Lionheart are displayed in the ambulatory. The 14th-century Lady Chapel has two impressive tombs: one to the cardinals of Amboise, both called Georges, who are shown on their knees dressed in rich robes and framed by a Renaissance frieze; the other to Louis de Brézé whose wife, Diane de Poitiers, mistress of Henri II (➤ 37), is shown grieving over her husband.

✝ 34B2
✉ place de la Cathédrale
☎ 02 35 89 73 78
🕐 Tue–Sun 8–6, Mon and civil hols 2–6. Guided tours daily (Sat, Sun in winter) 3
🍴 Palais de Justice
🚌 3, 13
♿ None
💶 Tours: moderate
↔ Rue du Gros-Horloge (➤ 26), Église St-Maclou (➤ 34)

Above: *the cardinals of Amboise, carved by Roulland le Roux on their 16th-century tomb*

MUSÉE DES ANTIQUITÉS ✪

Housed in a 17th-century convent, this extensive collection includes Egyptian, Greek, Gallo-Roman and medieval artefacts, including its star exhibit, the famous 4th-century Mosaic of Lillebonne, the largest in France. Tapestries, tiles, Renaissance furniture and carved Rouennais façades are also on display. The natural history and ethnography museum is next door.

✚ 35C3
✉ 198 rue Beauvoisine
☎ 02 35 98 55 10
🕐 Mon–Sat 10–12:15, 1:30–5:30, Sun 2–6
🚌 Beauvoisine
♿ Few
💲 Cheap

MUSÉE DES BEAUX-ARTS ✪✪

Paintings by Velázquez, Fragonard, Géricault, Caravaggio, David, Renoir and Monet are on view in this grand civic building that overlooks a small park and ornamental pond. The collection, spanning five centuries, takes in Russian icons, Impressionism and Raymond Duchamp-Villon's vigorous modern sculpture.

✚ 34B2
✉ square Verdrel
☎ 02 35 71 28 40
🕐 Wed–Mon 10–6
🚌 Beaux-Arts
💲 Moderate
❓ Ticket (panel, ▶ below)

MUSÉE DE LA CÉRAMIQUE ✪

In the 17th and 18th centuries Rouen acquired fame and fortune producing faïence, a style of tin-glazed earthenware with blue decoration on a white background or vice versa. Examples of this and other ceramics, including tableware and ornaments, are displayed in the 17th-century Hôtel d'Hocqueville, illustrating the industry's history.

✚ 34B2
✉ 1 rue Faucon
☎ 02 35 07 31 74
🕐 Wed–Mon 10–1, 2–6
🚇 Jeanne d'Arc
🚌 1, 2, 3, 4, 11, 13, 20, 22
♿ None
💲 Cheap
❓ Ticket (panel, ▶ below)

Did you know ?

A combined ticket allows admission to Tour du Beffroi (▶ 26), Musée des Beaux-Arts, Musée de la Céramique and Musée le Secq des Tournelles (▶ 34).

Ornate 18th-century faïence in the Musée de la Céramique

MUSÉE FLAUBERT ET D'HISTOIRE DE LA MÉDECINE ✪

This dual-purpose museum in the 18th-century Hôtel-Dieu has memorabilia of Gustave Flaubert in the room where he was born (his father was a surgeon here), and miscellaneous tools used in 19th-century hospitals. Exhibits include a childbirth demonstrator, surgical instruments and, for times when all else failed, statues of healing saints.

✚ 34A2
✉ 51 rue de Lecat
☎ 02 35 15 59 95
🕐 Tue 10–6, Wed–Sat 10–12, 2–6
🚌 Flaubert
♿ Few 💲 Free

33

An alfresco lunch on rue Damiette, between the churches of St-Maclou and St-Ouen

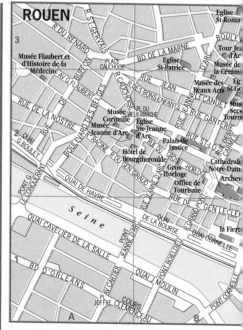

ROUEN

✚ 34B2
✉ 2 rue Jacques Villon
☎ 02 35 88 42 92
🕐 Wed–Sun 10–1, 2–6.
Closed Tue and some hols
🚇 Beaux-Arts
🚌 1, 2, 3, 4, 11, 13, 20, 22
✋ Cheap
❓ Ticket (panel, ▶ 33)

✚ 34B2
✉ rue aux Juifs
☎ 02 35 88 55 88
🕐 Wed 2–6, Thu–Mon 10–6
🚇 Palais de Justice
🚌 8, 2, 28
✋ Free
↔ Rue du Gros-Horloge
(▶ 26)

✚ 35C1
✉ place Barthélemy

MUSÉE LE SECQ DES TOURNELLES ⓞⓞ

The 15th-century Église St-Laurent, all flying buttresses and tracery, is an apt setting for one of Rouen's most intriguing museums. On display is a collection of wrought ironwork in every imaginable form, from an elegant 18th-century banister (taken from the Château de Bellevue) to the loops and swirls of old shop signs, keys, door knockers and painful-looking corsets.

PALAIS DE JUSTICE ⓞⓞ

When Normandy was granted its own *parlement* in 1514 the city's new exchequer building and merchants' hall was chosen to house the debating chamber and law court. It certainly provided due pomp and decoration: pinnacles, gargoyles, statuettes and tracery cluster about the steep-pitched, grey roofs in a Gothic frenzy. Excavations in the palace courtyard uncovered the Monument Juif (Jewish Monument), the remains of a late-11th-century synagogue.

RUE DU GROS-HORLOGE (▶ 26, TOP TEN)

ST-MACLOU, ÉGLISE ⓞⓞⓞ

Badly damaged during World War II, this extravagant Flamboyant church finally reopened in 1980 after years of careful restoration. It was built between 1437 and 1517,

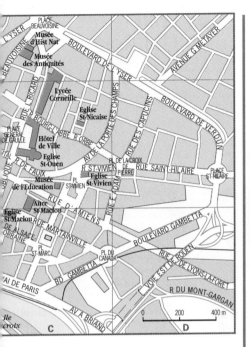

The 20m Croix de la Réhabilitation marks the scene of Joan of Arc's death (place du Vieux-Marché)

☎ 02 32 08 32 40 (Syndicat Initiative)

🕐 Aître courtyard daily 8–8

🍴 Palais de Justice

🚌 13, 3

🎟 Free

↔ Gros-Horloge (➤ 26), Cathédrale Notre-Dame (➤ 32)

dedicated to St Malo, a 7th-century missionary possibly of Welsh origin. Its wooden doors and stone porch are overwhelmed with carvings, some dating back to the 1550s, others decapitated deliberately. To the left of the porch a Renaissance fountain shows Bacchus flanked by two 'urinating' boys. Inside the church is a magnificent spiral staircase leading to the 16th-century organ case.

A short distance northeast from the church off rue Martainville is the Aître St-Maclou, a group of 16th-century timber-framed buildings around a courtyard. This was originally the parish charnel-house and now forms part of the Fine Arts School. The galleries are decorated with macabre carvings of skeletons, skulls and other *memento mori*. Immediately right of the entrance, behind a glass panel, is the skeletal mummy of a cat.

TOUR JEANNE D'ARC ✪

Only a massive round donjon, with 4m-thick walls and a witch's-hat roof, survives of the 13th-century fortress built by King Philippe Auguste. The name is slightly misleading: Jeanne d'Arc (Joan of Arc) was imprisoned in another tower and was only brought here to be shown the torture chamber as part of the attempt to break her spirit. The tower now houses documents about Joan's trial along with displays tracing the history of the region.

➕ 34B3

✉ rue du Donjon

☎ 02 35 98 16 21

🕐 Mon–Sat 10–12:30, 2–6 (5 Oct–Mar); Sun 2–6:30 (5:30 Oct–Mar)

🍴 Beaux-Arts

🚌 1, 2, 3, 4, 11, 13, 20, 22

🎟 Cheap

WALK

A Walk Around Old Rouen

Distance
About 2.5km

Time
1 hour, excluding visits

Start point
Cathédrale Notre-Dame
34B2
3, 13

End point
Place du Vieux-Marché
34B2
2, 12, 28

Lunch
La Taverne Walsheim (€€)
rue Martainville
02 35 98 27 50

This walk, starting at the cathedral, leads past some of the best architecture of the old town.

Turn right up rue St-Romain.

Medieval buildings are crammed along one side of the street; note Roussel's wrought-iron shopfront. At the archbishop's palace, opposite, Joan of Arc was condemned in 1431 and posthumously declared innocent 25 years later.

At place Barthélemy visit Église St-Maclou (➤ 34); then take rue Martainville and turn left at 186 for Aitre St-Maclou (➤ 35). Return to place Barthélemy and turn right up rue Damiette. Continue to place du Lt–Aubert and detour left up rue d'Amiens.

Spectacular Rubenesque figures and other statues adorn the walls of the Medical Laboratory and the building opposite.

Return to the square and continue along rue des Boucheries–St-Ouen, then turn right up rue Eau-de-Robec, where footbridges cross a narrow stream.

On the right, housed in a splendid medieval building, the Musée de l'Éducation illustrates the upbringing and education of children.

Cross place St-Vivien and continue along rue Eau-de-Robec to rue Édouard-Adam. Turn left and head for place de la Croix de Pierre; then turn left up rue St-Vivien.

Beyond place St-Vivien, the street leads past Église St-Ouen on the right and a huddle of narrow timber-framed houses on the left.

Timbered jetties above rue Martainville, near Église St-Maclou

Continue into rue de l'Hôpital and turn left on to rue des Carmes. Follow this to rue du Gros-Horloge. Turn right and continue under the Gros-Horloge (➤ 26) to place du Vieux-Marché.

What to See in the Northeast

Château d'Anet, with the clock gateway on the left

LES ANDELYS AND CHÂTEAU GAILLARD (► 17, TOP TEN)

ANET, CHÂTEAU D' ✪✪

In 1531 the future King Henri II, then just 12 years old, fell under the spell of Diane de Poitiers, the beautiful 32-year-old widow of Louis de Brézé, the former Lord of Anet. She became his mistress, and when Henri died in 1559 Diane retired to her château – a glorious showplace. Celebrated craftsmen worked here, including Benvenuto Cellini; Philibert Delorme designed the gateway and its extraordinary clock, with hounds that once barked the hour and a stag that stamped its hoof. Tours include the state rooms and chapel, adorned with golden globes.

✚ 41B1
☎ 02 37 41 90 07
🕐 Apr–Oct, Wed–Sun 2–6:30; Nov, Feb–Mar, Sat, Sun 2–5. Closed Dec, Jan
🍴 Restaurants in Anet (€–€€)
🚌 From Dreux
💰 Expensive

ARQUES-LA-BATAILLE ✪

The donjon and walls of an 11th-century fortress dominate this riverside town. The battle referred to in the place name was in 1589, when Protestant Henri IV saw off the superior forces of the Catholic League. Despite the siege and stone robbing the ruins are still impressive; the gatehouse shows a carved relief of the battle. The town's 16th-century Église Notre-Dame de l'Assomption has a bust of Henri IV.

✚ 39C2
🍴 Choice in Dieppe (€€–€€€), or Manoir d'Archelles, south on D1 near Martigny (€–€€)
🚌 From Dieppe and Rouen
🔁 Dieppe (► 21)

CAUDEBEC-EN-CAUX ✪

Extending along a wide stretch of the Seine, Caudebec has the air of a minor seaside resort, with shops and restaurants lining the waterfront. The Flamboyant Église Notre-Dame stands in the market place amid modern apartment blocks and shops. The **Maison des Templiers**, a 13th-century stone building, houses a local history display, and the Musée de la Marine de Seine looks at river navigation through the ages. Just outside the town the nose and wing of a stone biplane protrude from a rock, a memorial to five aviators who disappeared in the 1920s en route to the Arctic to rescue Italian balloonists who had crashed near Spitzbergen.

✚ 38B1
🍴 Restaurants (€€–€€€)
🚌 From Rouen and Le Havre

Maison des Templiers
✉ rue Thomas Basin
☎ 02 39 96 95 91
🕐 May, Oct, Wed, Sun 3:30–6:30, Sat 10–12, 3:30–6; Jun, Sep, Mon, Fri, Sat 10–12, 3:30–6, Sun 3:30–6:30; Jul–Aug, Fri–Wed 10–12, 3:30–6
💰 Cheap

37

+ 39C1

¶¶ Choice of restaurants
(€–€€)

🚌 From Rouen

Parc Zoologique

☎ 02 35 33 23 08

🕐 Mar–Sep, daily 10–7; Oct
10–5:30, Nov 1:30–5

♿ Few

✋ Moderate

+ 41B3

¶¶ None in village

↔ Les Andelys (▶ 17),
Lyons-la-Forêt (▶ 43)

CLÈRES

A large covered market hall forms the centre of this quiet village, but the main attraction lies to the west where the 19th-century neo-Gothic Château de Clères stands on the site of an 11th-century stronghold. Since 1920 its grounds have been given over to the **Parc Zoologique** whose inhabitants include flamingos, emus, peacocks, kangaroos and antelopes. The Musée de l'Automobile has a collection of vintage cars ranging from the late 19th to the early 20th centuries, as well as cycles and military vehicles from World War II.

DIEPPE (▶ 21, TOP TEN)

ÉCOUIS

Planted incongruously in the middle of this unremarkable village is the twin-towered collegiate church of Notre-Dame, visible from afar across the flat countryside. Built in the early 14th century by King Philip IV's finance minister, Enguerrand de Marigny, it has a wonderfully spacious interior lit by two large stained-glass transept windows. Look out for the brick vault and intricately carved bosses in the side chapel, carved doors and wooden ceiling in the enclosed chapel near the entrance, and timber spiral stairs leading to the organ loft.

Exotic cranes wander freely on the lawns around the Château de Clères

NORTHEAST NORMANDY

ÉTRETAT ✪✪✪

Étretat is the most attractive Norman resort north of
Honfleur and is always busy in summer. Out of season it
carries on a quiet but cheerful life of its own.

The shingle beach stretches between two glaring chalk
headlands, both sculpted by the elements. The Falaise
d'Aval (western cliff) ends in a wide and fragile-looking
arch, a flying buttress against the main body of rock. The
eastern cliff, the Falaise d'Amont, is less dramatic.
Perched on top of it is the seamen's chapel of Notre-
Dame-de-la-Garde, and a monument commemorating
Charles Nungesser and François Coli, French aviators who
set out from Paris in 1927 to try and cross the Atlantic to
New York in their 'Oiseau Blanc'; they were last seen over
this part of the coast. There is also a museum with
mementoes of the pilots.

The centre of the town is full of character. In place du
Maréchal Foch 16th-century town houses are grouped
around the wooden *halles* (covered market), where in
summer souvenir shops open under the first-floor
galleries; over the entrance to the *halles* is an unusual
carving of a bat with a man's head. A plaque beneath the
clock tower in the *place* commemorates Étretat's World
War I field hospital, and the arrival of Scottish troops in
World War II.

🚩 38A2
🍴 Choice of restaurants
(€–€€€)
⬌ Fécamp (➤ 40)

*The natural chalk arch of
the Falaise d'Aval
Insert: aviators
Nungesser and Coli*

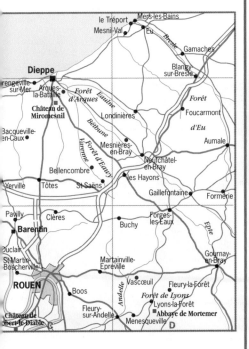

+ 39D3

†| Hôtel de la Gare, 20
avenue de la Gare (€–€€)

🚌 From Rouen/Dieppe

↔ Le Tréport (▶ 45)

Musée Louis-Philippe

☎ 02 35 86 04 68

🕐 Mid-Mar to 5 Nov,
Wed–Mon 10–12, 2–6

🚻 Good

💷 Moderate

+ 38A2

†| Choice of restaurants on
quays (€–€€)

🚌 60/61 from Dieppe, 26B
from Rouen

↔ 7 a day from Rouen

↔ Étretat (▶ 39)

Palais Bénédictine

✉ 110 rue Alexandre-le-
Grand

☎ 02 35 10 26 10

🕐 Feb–Mar, Nov, Dec, daily
10:30–11:45, 2–5;
Apr–mid-Jul, Sep, Oct,
daily 10–12, 2–5:30; mid-
Jul–Aug, daily
10–6

🚻 Few

💷 Moderate

EU ✪

Set on the Bresle river, with the Forêt d'Eu spreading towards the southeast, this once powerful *ville royale* has two buildings out of proportion to the small centre. The grandiose red-brick and stone Château d'Eu, on the site of an older fortress where William the Conqueror was married, was the favoured home of King Louis-Philippe and houses the **Musée Louis-Philippe**. Facing it is the medieval Église Notre-Dame et St-Laurent that houses the remains of Saint Laurence O'Toole, a 12th-century archbishop of Dublin.

FÉCAMP ✪✪

This workaday harbour town is the home of Bénédictine liqueur, made from a secret recipe discovered by Alexandre le Grand in a 16th-century monastic manuscript. Le Grand promoted the product with gusto, commissioning posters by celebrated artists and building the neo-Gothic **Palais Bénédictine**. This now contains an art gallery and museum, as well as the copper Bénédictine stills; tours and tastings are provided.

For centuries Fécamp was a major centre of pilgrimage and people flocked to the monastery to see the relic of the Precious Blood of Christ; it was supposedly washed ashore in a hollow fig tree and is now housed in the beautiful 12th- to 13th-century Église de La Trinité.

PALAIS
BÉNÉDICTINE
usée & Distillerie
Centre Culturel
Boutique
VISITE TOUS LES JOURS

Copper stills in Fécamp's Palais Bénédictine

Did you know?

Eu was an important administrative town until the 15th century, when Louis XI took drastic action to prevent its fall into English hands. He had everything except the churches burned to the ground, and the town never recovered its former glory.

GISORS ✪

The capital of the Normandie-Vexin stands on rising ground beside the region's eastern border, amid seemingly endless flatlands. Behind the main street are the ruins of a 12th-century fortress, where a slender donjon was built by King Henry II of England; it is surrounded by moss-covered walls and a filled-in ditch where locals now play *boules*. King Philippe Auguste added the Tour du Prisonnier, which became a prison in the 16th century – drawings and inscriptions by the inmates can still be seen. Across town the church of St-Gervais and St-Protais contains an impressive Tree of Jesse.

🏠 41C3
🍴 Choice of restaurants (€€–€€€)
🚌 2 a day from Évreux

SEINE VALLEY

ROUEN · Martainville-Epreville · Château de Martainville · Andelle · Vascœuil · Fleury-la-Forêt · Gournay-en-Bray · Beauvais

Boos · Forêt de Lyons · Lyons-la-Forêt

Abbaye de Fontaine-Guérard · Menesqueville · Abbaye de Mortemer · Auneuil

Château de Robert-le-Diable · Fleury-sur-Andelle · Bonnemare

Seine · Côte des Deux Amants · Ecouis

Pont-de-l'Arche · les Andelys · Gisors

Elbeuf · le Vaudreuil · Château Gaillard · les Thilliers-en-Vexin

Louviers · Lierville

Gaillon · Epte · Magny-en-Vexin · Marines

Vernon · Giverny · Bonnières-sur-Seine · Pontoise

Château de Bizy · Pacy-sur-Eure · Meulan

Evreux · Eure · Chaufour-les-Bonnières · Limay · Seine · Les Mureaux

Mantes-la-Jolie · Flins-sur-Seine

Iton · Epône

St-Andre-de-l'Eure · Ivry-la-Bataille · Maule · Orgeval · St-Germain-en-Laye

Damville · Anet · Château d'Anet · Vesgre · Houdan · Pontchartrain

St-Lubin-des-Joncherets · Avre · Montfort-l'Amaury

Dreux · 0 10 20 km · Chevreuse

A · B · C

41

🕂 41B2
🍴 Les Jardins de Giverny at
   Musée d'Art Américain
   (€€). Closed Feb
🚇 From Vernon station

Jardins Monet
✉ On the D313
☎ 02 32 51 28 21
🕐 Apr–Oct, Tue–Sun
   9:30–6. Also Easter and
   Whit Monday
♿ Few
💷 Expensive

🕂 38A1
🍴 Choice of restaurants in
   Ste-Addresse area
   (€€–€€€)
🚇 From Caen, Lisieux and
   Caudebec-en-Caux
   (connection with Rouen)
🚂 11 a day from Rouen
🔁 Le Havre (► 22, Top Ten)

Musée de l'Ancien Havre
✉ 1 rue Jérôme Bellarmato
☎ 02 35 42 27 90
🕐 Wed–Sun 10–12, 2–6
♿ None
💷 Cheap

*Reflections on the water-
lily pond at Giverny*

GIVERNY ✪✪
Visitors come to this riverside hamlet to see Claude Monet's house and the gardens that he created and later painted (► 14). Footpaths lead round the gardens, which are very beautiful but inevitably obscured by the crowds. The most popular photo opportunity is the water-lily pond and its bridge, familiar from Monet's famous series of paintings. A road through the **Jardins Monet** divides the Clos Normand (enclosed garden) from the Water Garden. The artist's 'pink house' has reproductions of his works, Japanese engravings, and rooms decorated in different colours. The Musée d'Art Américain, near by, celebrates the works of American artists past and present.

LE HAVRE ✪
From the Pont de Normandie and the east, traffic enters Le Havre past petrochemical factories into a maze of low apartment blocks and shops. This is the modern centre designed by Auguste Perret after the old town was levelled in World War II. One of the few pre-war survivors is the 17th-century building housing the **Musée de l'Ancien Havre**, a token of the town's former character.

Le Havre has a long seafaring pedigree, but rather than try to recapture the past Perret went for unapologetic modernism. Beyond the *bassin du commerce* (commercial dock), crossed by an elegant white bridge, a ship's funnel rises from the underground bowl of Espace Oscar Niemeyer, home of Le Volcan arts centre. Inside Perret's monumental Église St-Joseph to the west, light sparkles through the stained glass of the 109m octagonal lantern tower to the semi-darkness within. To the south, the 16th-century Cathédrale Notre-Dame is an eccentric mix of architectural styles.

HONFLEUR (▶ 23, TOP TEN)

JUMIÈGES, ABBAYE DE (▶ 16, TOP TEN)

LYONS-LA-FORÊT ✪✪✪

Huddled in a dip of the Lieure Valley, Lyons-la-Forêt is a classic Norman timber-framed village, where narrow 17th-century buildings crowd round the old *halles*. A wonderful old house downhill from the market square, topped with decorative ceramic chimney pots, has a plaque stating that Maurice Ravel composed *Le Tombeau de Couperin* there in 1917. These houses and the 12th-century Église St-Denis are the only sights as such, but the prettiness of this picture-postcard village makes it a popular base for exploring the surrounding Forêt de Lyons.

Among the slender beeches – which filter an ethereal light even into the heart of the forest – is the Abbaye de Mortemer, ruins of a medieval Cistercian abbey with a museum of monastic life. Here also are the Château de Fleury-la-Forêt with its collection of toys and dolls, and the **Château de Vascœuil** on the forest's edge, with reconstructions of traditional cottages in its grounds.

🗺 39D1
🍴 La Licorne (€€–€€€)
🚌 From Rouen
↔ Écouis (▶ 38)

Château de Vascœuil
☎ 02 35 23 62 35
🍴 Restaurant La Cascade (€€), in the Chateau
🕐 Mid-Apr–Jun, Sep–mid-Oct, Mon–Sat 2:30–6:30, Sun 11–7; Jul, Aug, daily 11–7
💰 Expensive

The timber halles *at Lyons-la-Forêt*

MARTAINVILLE, CHÂTEAU DE ✪

Privateer Jacques le Pelletier built this château in the late 15th century, and his nephew later transformed it from a fortified house into a stately home. Its round, red-brick towers are topped with conical roofs and there is a large 16th-century dovecote in the grounds. Inside is the Musée Départemental des Traditions et Arts Normands, with a collection of furniture, ceramics, glass and costumes.

🗺 41A3
✉ 16km east of Rouen
☎ 02 35 23 44 70
🕐 Wed–Mon 10–12:30, 2–6 (till 5 in winter). Closed Tue and Sun am
🍴 Restaurants in village (€€)
🚌 28A from Rouen
💰 Moderate

MIROMESNIL, CHÂTEAU DE ✪

Guy de Maupassant (1850–93) was born in this 16th-century red-brick and stone château. Memorabilia associated with the writer are displayed inside, as well as books collected by the Marquis de Miromesnil, Louis XVI's chancellor, who died here in 1796. A 16th-century chapel with an ornate interior stands in the grounds.

🗺 39C2
✉ Tourville-sur-Arques
☎ 02 35 80 02 80
🕐 May–Sep, Wed–Mon 2–6
🚌 From Dieppe (summer)
💰 Expensive

🚻 38B1
🍴 Choice of cafés
and restaurants
(€–€€)
🚌 From Lisieux or
Rouen

*Goods change
hands at Pont-
Audemer's busy
market*

PONT-AUDEMER ⚫⚫

Pont-Audemer's prosperity was built on its tanneries, and it retains the air of a working town. Situated between two branches of the Risle river, the modern shops and houses blend with narrow alleyways and court-yards lined with historic buildings. Canals cut through town, crossed by wooden footbridges, and there are good examples of 17th-century housing along rue de la République, Cour Canel and near the 11th-century Église St-Ouen.

🚻 39C1
✉ 10km northwest of
Rouen off D982
☎ 02 35 32 10 82
🍴 Bars near the church (€)
🚌 From Rouen
♿ Few; difficult access to
church
🎟 Moderate

ST-MARTIN-DE-BOSCHERVILLE ⚫⚫

This tiny village is dominated by the former abbey church, now the parish church of St-Georges-de-Boscherville. Refounded as a Benedictine monastery in 1144, it housed a small community of monks until they fled during the Revolution. Wide steps ascend to the church's simple Romanesque façade, built of gleaming limestone with a fine doorway. Inside, the space and light created by its austere design is breathtaking; look for the puppet-like carvings on the transept columns.

🚻 38B1
✉ 30km west of Rouen, off
D982
☎ 02 35 96 23 11
🕐 Guided tours of cloisters
Apr–Oct Mon–Fri 3:30;
Nov–Mar Sat 3:30, Sun
and hols (not Mon) 11:30,
3:30. Closed Mon, Easter
Sun, 25 Dec
🍴 Auberge Deux Couronnes
(€€); tearooms in village
(€€)
🚌 From Rouen
♿ None
🎟 Moderate (for tour)
🚂 Caudebec-en-Caux

*Benedictine monks
enter the precinct of
St-Wandrille*

ST-WANDRILLE, ABBAYE DE ⚫

In 628 Count Wandrille renounced the secular world and after stops at various monasteries founded his own in the Seine Valley. It soon gained a reputation for scholarship but had to be rebuilt after Viking raids. The abbey passed into private hands after the French Revolution until 1931 when the Benedictine community was re-established. Remains of the 14th-century abbey church and cloister can be seen in the grounds, as well as a 13th-century tithe barn rebuilt by the monks in 1967.

The impressive columns of the Abbaye de St-Wandrille tower above visitors

LE TRÉPORT ⭐

The bracing seaside resort of le Tréport lies on the region's windswept northeastern corner. High chalk cliffs shelter a shingle beach and provide views from the Calvaire des Terrasses. The restored 16th-century Église St-Jacques at the end of quai François 1er overlooks the harbour and fishing boats; its 11th-century predecessor disappeared with former cliffs into the sea.

VALMONT ⭐

From the flint and brick church at the centre of this small country town you can look up at the high, buttressed walls and slate roofs of the château established by the powerful Estouteville family. In 1169 Nicolas d'Estouteville founded the Benedictine **abbey** whose ruins stand at the foot of a wooded slope. They include the 16th-century choir, and the graceful Chapelle de la Vierge, or Six Heures (the time of the daily mass), that houses the tombs of Jacques d'Estouteville and the abbey's founder; five 15th-century windows depict the life of the Virgin.

🔲 39D3
🍴 Choice of cafés and seafood restaurants along quai François 1er (€€)
🚌 From Rouen and Dieppe
🔄 Eu (► 40)

🔲 38B2
🍴 Auberge du Bec au Cauchois, 1.5km west (€–€€)
🚌 From Rouen

Abbaye
☎ 02 35 27 34 92
🕐 Guided tours: Apr–Sep, Wed–Mon 2–5
🎟 Free

A Drive Along the Côte d'Albâtre

Distance
80km

Time
2½ hours excluding visits

Start point
Dieppe
✚ 39C2

End point
Étretat
✚ 38A2

Lunch
Le Relais des Dalles (€€)
✉ 6 rue Elisabeth
d'Autriche, Sassetot-le-
Mauconduit
☎ 02 35 27 41 83

This coastal drive detours inland to explore the Pays de Caux.

From Dieppe take the D75 signed St-Valéry-en-Caux.

The road twists down into the breezy resort of Pourville-sur-Mer, with panoramic sea views.

Continue along the D75 through Varengeville-sur-Mer (➤ 47) to Ste-Marguerite-sur-Mer.

Stop here to look at the 12th- to 16th-century church. To the right of the entrance is a carving of an owl holding a snake in its beak; owl motifs are repeated on columns in the dark interior.

At St-Aubin-sur-Mer follow the coast to Veules-les-Roses; turn right on to the D925 (St-Valéry-en-Caux). Take the D925 towards Fécamp and turn on to the D68 (signed St-Sylvain). The road passes through a broad, flat landscape with an aerodrome in the distance, before descending through beech woods into Paluel. Continue to St-Martin-aux-Buneaux and take the D68 to Sassetot-le-Mauconduit.

High and dry on the beach near Yport

At Malleville-les-Grès, beyond Paluel, the D68 passes a handsome manor house and a 1650 stone cross. Next, a turreted wall surrounds the lordly 15th-century château at Auberville-la-Manuel. Facing the road at Sassetot is a pink and white château, now a hotel.

Follow signs to Valmont (➤ 45). Take the D150 to Fécamp (➤ 40), then the D940 and D104 to Yport. From Yport, with its impressive red-brick and limestone church, the D211 winds through woodland, overlooking the sea, to Vattetot-sur-Mer. At Vattetot turn right on to the D11 and descend into a green valley on the approach to Étretat.

VARENGEVILLE-SUR-MER ★

The wooded coast road runs southwest of Dieppe through a series of townships that make up Varengeville. Just inland the privateer-politician Jean Ango built his summer palace, the **Manoir d'Ango**, in 1530, decorating it with busts of the great and good, including François I and himself.

Closer to the coast, the gardens of the **Parc Floral du Bois des Moutiers** include rhododendrons and magnolias among the shrubs offering spring colour. Formal flower beds are arranged around a house built in 1898 from the designs of the English architect Edwin Lutyens. In the town's cliff-top church is a stunning stained-glass Tree of Jesse by Georges Braque; the cubist painter came to live here in 1930.

Braque's vivid Tree of Jesse window in the church at Varengeville

🗺️ 39C2
🍴 Hôtel de la Terrasse (€–€€)
🚌 From Dieppe
↔️ Dieppe (▶ 21)

Manoir d'Ango
✉️ 7km west of Dieppe
☎️ 02 35 85 14 80
🕐 Mar–Nov, Tue–Sun and public hols 10–12:30, 2–6:30
🎫 Moderate

Parc Floral du Bois des Moutiers
✉️ 78km west of Dieppe
☎️ 02 35 85 10 02
🕐 Mid-Mar to mid-Nov, daily 10–12, 2–6
🎫 Expensive for tours of gardens plus house

VERNON ★

Vernon is a bustling market town on the Seine. Many of its medieval buildings survive, one of the best, with faded 15th-century carvings, housing the tourist office on rue Carnot; the nearby Gothic church has striking abstract stained-glass windows. The massive circular donjon visible from the rue du Vieux Château was once part of the castle built by King Philippe Auguste. Across the river, near the miniature Château des Tourelles, a timber-framed house perches on a stump of the former medieval bridge.

Just outside Vernon the 18th-century **Château de Bizy**, set in terraced gardens, has a fine collection of tapestries.

🗺️ 41B2
🍴 Restaurants (€–€€€)
🚌 From Évreux

Château de Bizy
✉️ 2km south of Vernon
☎️ 02 32 51 00 82
🕐 Apr–Oct, Tue–Sun 10–12, 2–6; Nov, Feb–Mar, weekend 2–5. Closed Dec–Jan
🎫 Expensive

Caen & Central Normandy

Central Normandy is composed of a variety of landscapes, from the D-Day beaches and seaside resorts of the Côte Fleurie and the Côte de Nacre, to the quiet towns of the rural south.

Between the coast and the distant Loire region are the lush fields, dairy farms and orchards of the Pays d'Auge around Lisieux, the gentle Pays d'Ouche south of Bernay, and the rich meadows of the Perche region, famous for its horses. To the the west, the rocky gorges and wooded hills of the Suisse Normande are perfect for hiking, walking and canoeing.

As well as the traditional timber-framed buildings, there are churches and houses of mellow, creamy limestone; this same material was once shipped from the busy port of Caen to build new cathedrals in the Norman-ruled kingdom of England.

> ‘… the most prepossessing … and most happily situated of towns … and from this town have come the brightest wits and intelligences of their country.’
>
> MADAME DE SÉVIGNÉ,
> of Caen in 1689

Opposite: *Abbaye aux Hommes, Caen*

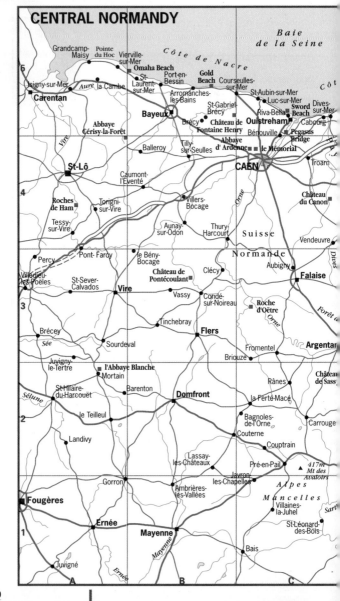

CENTRAL NORMANDY

Baie de la Seine

Côte de Nacre

Grandcamp-Maisy
Pointe du Hoc
Vierville-sur-Mer
Omaha Beach
Port-en-Bessin
Gold Beach
Courseulles-sur-Mer
Côt

Isigny-sur-Mer
Aure
la Cambe
St-Laurent-sur-Mer
Arromanches-les-Bains
St-Aubin-sur-Mer
Luc-sur-Mer
Riva-Bella
Sword Beach
Dives-sur-Mer

Carentan

Bayeux
St-Gabriel-Brécy
Ouistreham
Cabourg

Abbaye Cérisy-la-Forêt
Brécy
Château de Fontaine Henry
Bénouville
Pegasus Bridge

Vire
Balleroy
Tilly-sur-Seulles
Abbaye d' Ardenne
le Mémorial

St-Lô
Caumont-l'Éventé
CAEN
Troarn

Roches de Ham
Torigni-sur-Vire
Villers-Bocage
Orne
Château du Canon

Tessy-sur-Vire
Aunay-sur-Odon
Thury-Harcourt
Suisse
Vendeuvre

Percy
Pont-Farcy
le Bény-Bocage
Norma n de
Aubigny
Falaise

Villedieu-les-Poêles
St-Sever-Calvados
Château de Pontécoulant
Clécy
Dites

Vire
Vassy
Condé-sur-Noireau
Roche d'Oëtre
Forêt d

Brécey
Sée
Sourdeval
Tinchebray
Flers
Orne

Juvigny-le-Tertre
l'Abbaye Blanche
Mortain
Fromentel
Argentan

St-Hilaire-du-Harcouët
Barenton
Briouze
Rânes
Château de Sass

Séune
le Teilleul
Domfront
la-Ferté-Macé

Landivy
Bagnoles-de-l'Orne
Carrouge

Couterne
Couptrain

Lassay-les-Châteaux
Pré-en-Pail
▲ 417m Mt des Avaloirs

Gorron
Javron-les-Chapelles
Alpes

Ambrières-les-Vallées
M a n c e l l e s
Villaines-la-Juhel
Sart

Fougères

Ernée
Mayenne
Mayenne
St-Léonard-des-Bois

Bais

Juvigné
Ernée

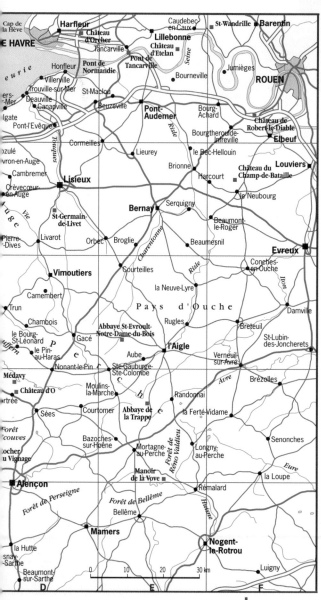

Cap de la Hève
Harfleur
Château d'Orcher
E HAVRE
Tancarville
Pont de Tancarville
Caudebec-en-Caux
St-Wandrille
Barentin
Lillebonne
Château d'Etelan
Pont de Normandie
Honfleur
Villerville
Trouville-sur-Mer
St-Maclou
ers-Mer
Deauville
Canapville
Igate
Pont-l'Évêque
Beuzeville
Seine
Bourneville
Jumièges
ROUEN
Bourg-Achard
Bourgtheroulde-Infreville
Château de Robert-le-Diable
Elbeuf
Pont-Audemer
Risle
ozulé
vron-en-Auge
Cormeilles
Lieurey
le Bec-Hellouin
Louviers
Cambremer
Brionne
Harcourt
Château du Champ-de-Bataille
Crèvecœur-en-Auge
Touques
Lisieux
le Neubourg
uge
Vie
St-Germain-de-Livet
Bernay
Serquigny
Beaumont-le-Roger
Pierre-Dives
Livarot
Orbec
Broglie
Charentonne
Beaumesnil
Evreux
Vimoutiers
Courteilles
Risle
Conches-en-Ouche
Iton
la Neuve-Lyre
Camembert
Pays d'Ouche
Damville
Trun
Chambois
Rugles
Breteuil
St-Lubin-des-Joncherets
le Bourg-St-Léonard
Gacé
Abbaye St-Evroult-Notre-Dame-du-Bois
l'Aigle
le Pin-au-Haras
Aube
Ste-Gauburge-Ste-Colombe
Verneuil-sur-Avre
Médavy
Nonant-le-Pin
Château d'O
Moulins-la-Marche
Avre
Brézolles
rtrée
Sées
Courtomer
Abbaye de la Trappe
Randonnai
la Ferté-Vidame
Forêt couves
Bazoches-sur-Hoëne
Mortagne-au-Perche
Senonches
ocher u Vignage
Longny-au-Perche
Forêt de Réno Valdieu
Eure
Manoir de la Vove
la Loupe
Alençon
Forêt de Perseigne
Rémalard
Forêt de Bellême
Bellême
Huisne
la Hutte
snay-Sarthe
Mamers
Nogent-le-Rotrou
Beaumont-sur-Sarthe
Luigny

0   10   20   30 km

D   E   F

51

Some of the older houses that survived the battle for Caen during June and July 1944

Caen

Traffic roars around Caen's floodlit medieval château, which, along with the Église St-Pierre opposite its town gate, provides the main focus of this busy river port. Three-quarters of the city were destroyed during World War II, but the modern, businesslike centre still retains a few old buildings in golden Caen limestone. On the outskirts, the cost and legacy of war are considered in the remarkable Mémorial (➤ 19).

What to See in Caen

ABBAYE AUX DAMES ⚫

Duke William, later Conqueror, defied a papal ruling to marry his distant cousin, Matilda of Flanders, and both were excommunicated in 1051. Eight years later, Abbot Lanfranc of Bec persuaded the Pope to lift the exclusion in return for the founding of two abbeys: the Abbaye aux Dames, northeast of the centre, where Matilda would be interred, and the Abbaye aux Hommes, William's mausoleum. Matilda's simple black-marble tomb lies in the chancel of the abbey church, La Trinité.

ABBAYE AUX HOMMES ⚫⚫

Viewed from the east across a geometric formal garden, the abbey buildings and Église St-Étienne present a striking mixture of styles. To the left are the classical 18th-century monastic buildings, now housing the town hall; to the right the chancel of the abbey church, busy with early Gothic spires, turrets and buttresses. The original west façade is simpler, its elegant 11th-century towers crowned in the 13th century with octagonal spires. The Conqueror's fragmentary remains – one thigh bone – lie under an inscribed stone by the altar; the rest were stolen when Huguenots raided the church in the 16th century.

➕ 50C4

✉ place de la Reine Mathilde
☎ 02 31 06 98 98
🕐 Guided tours: daily 2:30, 4. Closed 1 Jan, 1 May, 25 Dec
♿ Good
🎫 Free

✉ esplanade Jean-Marie Louvel
☎ 02 31 30 42 81
🕐 Mon–Fri 8–6, Sat, Sun 8–5. Guided tours: daily 9:30, 11, 2:30, 4. Closed 1 Jan, 1 May, 25 Dec
♿ None
🎫 Cheap

CHÂTEAU ✪✪

Another of Duke William's foundations, the château was strengthened and embellished over several centuries. Its massive donjon was only destroyed during the Revolution, and more followed during World War II, but the restored walls are still impressive, situated on a rocky eminence surrounded by a grassed-over moat. Within the walls are the **Musée des Beaux-Arts** with its fine collection of 16th- to 17th-century Flemish, French and Italian paintings, and the **Musée de Normandie** (in the former governor's residence) that traces the region's history.

✉ rue Montoir-Poissonnerie, entry through Porte sur la Ville
💷 Free

Musée des Beaux-Arts
✉ Château precinct
☎ 02 31 30 47 70
🕐 Wed–Mon 9:30–6. Closed 1 Jan, Easter, 1 May, Ascension, 11 Nov, 25 Dec
♿ Good, some sections inaccessible
💷 Moderate; free Wed

Musée de Normandie
✉ Château precinct
☎ 02 31 30 47 60
🕐 Wed–Mon 9:30–6
♿ None
💷 Cheap; free Sun

The restored 12th-century walls of Caen's mighty château

ST-PIERRE, ÉGLISE ✪✪

St-Pierre's 72m spire provides a useful landmark within the town's confusing road system. There has been a church on the site since the 7th century, but the present building is mainly 13th- to 16th-century. There are some fine carvings inside, particularly on the columns on the northern side of the nave; medieval scenes here include a phoenix rising from the ashes, a unicorn comforted by a young woman, and the trials of the Knights of the Round Table.

✉ rue Montoir-Poissonnerie
🍴 Choice of restaurants, cafés and bars (€–€€€)

53

A Walk Around Caen's Monuments

Distance
About 5km

Time
1½ hours without visits

Start point
Abbaye aux Dames

End point
Abbaye aux Hommes

Lunch
Alcide (€€)
✉ 1 place Courtonne, Caen
☎ 02 31 94 47 45

Fourteenth-century vaulting in the Église St-Pierre, rebuilt after the devastation of 1944

This walk takes you from Mathilde's resting-place, Abbaye aux Dames, to that of William the Conqueror, visiting the main monuments and streets between the mausoleum churches.

Leaving the abbey church of La Trinité (place de la Reine Mathilde, ➤ 52), turn left and go down rue Manissier. At the end turn right on to rue Basse and continue to the pedestrian crossing; then turn left (rue Samuel Bochard) to reach place Courtonne.

Hotels and restaurants line this large open square that takes in the yachting marina and port at one end, and the lone Tour Guillaume-le-Roy at the other.

Turn right along rue des Prairies St-Gilles to rejoin rue Basse, then right up rue Buquet. Cross into rue du Vaugueux.

Some of Caen's most atmospheric restaurants can be found in this secluded cobbled area, one of the few surviving old streets.

At the end of the street cross the road to the castle: enter the grounds over the long drawbridge. Exit from the Musée des Beaux-Arts to Église St-Pierre (➤ 53), and cross into rue St-Pierre.

The Musée de la Poste, on this bustling shopping street, occupies the best example of timber-framed architecture in the city centre .

Just beyond the Église St-Sauveur (also known as Notre-Dame de Froide-rue), turn right into rue Froide. Continue to rue St-Sauveur and (left) place St-Sauveur.

Elegant town houses lead from Vieux St-Sauveur, a medieval church gradually being restored after extensive wartime damage, to the Palais de Justice whose classical columns dominate place Fontette.

Cross the square to the formal gardens for a magnificent view of Duke William's Abbaye aux Hommes (➤ 52).

What to See in Central Normandy

ALENÇON ✪

Alençon is a pleasant, unspoiled town of narrow streets and squares, whose centre is dominated by the neo-classical Palais de Justice and the grim château gatehouse. The nearby market hall is a striking circular, glass-domed building. The town made a name for itself when Louis XIV's minister Colbert established a lace industry here. Samples of Alençon lace are shown in the Musée des Beaux-Arts et de la Dentelle, a former Jesuit college.

+ 51D1
🍴 Choice of restaurants (€€)
🚌 From Argentan
🚂 Four per day from Rouen, Cherbourg
↔ Carrouges (▶ 61), Mortagne-au-Perche (▶ 67), Sées (▶ 74)

ARGENTAN ✪

Argentan provides a good touring centre for excursions into the wooded Suisse Normande. The town itself, which once rivalled Alençon's lace industry, has an impressive Flamboyant church – St-Germain – that stands opposite the turreted 14th-century château (now housing law courts); standing apart from the château is its former chapel, now the tourist information centre. The town was the scene of historic talks in the late 12th century, with papal legates trying to reconcile King Henry II of England and Thomas à Becket; when they failed, Henry's knights set off from Argentan to rid him of his 'turbulent priest'.

+ 50C3
🍴 Restaurants in town (€–€€)
🚌 From Alençon
🚂 Four per day from Rouen, four per day from Granville (Paris Montparnasse–Granville line)
↔ Château d'O (▶ 20), Château de Sassy (▶ 73)

ARROMANCHES-LES-BAINS ✪✪

Fragments of the artificial harbour 'Mulberry B' form a vast semicircle in the sea beyond this quiet seaside resort, a reminder of the D-Day landings of June 1944. Chunks of the harbour also lie on the sandy beach, giving an idea of the sheer size and scale of the operation, an account of which is given in the Musée du Débarquement. Visit the excellent 360° cinema that recreates the landings.

+ 50B5
🍴 Choice of cafés and brasseries (€–€€)
🚌 From Bayeux
↔ Bayeux (▶ 18, 57)

Above: *remains of the Mulberry harbour lie offshore at Arromanches*

55

A Drive Through Southern Forests

Distance
About 205km

Time
3½–4 hours without stops

Start/end point
Alençon
✚ 51D1

Lunch
Le Grenier à Sel (££)
✉ 9 rue Contcacune,
Mortane au Perche
☎ 02 33 25 51 98

This long circular drive passes through the Parc Naturel Régional Normandie-Maine and southern Normandy's ancient forests.

From Alençon, take the D311 east through the Forêt de Perseigne. At the roundabout before Mamers follow signs for Bellême (D311/D955).

Beyond the woods the road leads through gentle countryside into the Perche, with its extensive fields and pasture.

At the roundabout before Bellême turn left on to the D938 through the Forêt de Bellême, heading north to Mortagne–au–Perche. Beyond Mortagne's market hall turn right (D8).

The route passes through hamlets, pastureland and the Forêt de Réno-Valdieu to Longny-au-Perche. Here, a long flight of steps leads to the 16th-century Chapelle de Notre-Dame de Pitié, and the 16th-century tower of Église St-Martin overlooks the central square.

In the centre turn left (D918) to pass through the Forêt du Perche to Randonnai. Turn left at the traffic lights (D603).

The road leads between the Forêts du Perche and de la Trappe; a series of lakes can be glimpsed through the trees. A crucifix stands above the road as it reaches a fork. Take the right fork (Rond de Trappe), but be careful: deer are still hunted here.

Emerging on to the D930, turn right, then first left to the Abbaye de la Trappe.

Founded in 1140, the abbey has an audio-visual display describing the life of Trappist monks.

One of the peaceful roads that weave through the forests of Normandy

Turn left on a minor road to Prépotin; then left to a T-junction and right (D930). Turn right on to the N12. At the roundabout join the D8 to Sées (▶ 74). Take the D908 to a crossroads and turn left (D26) through the Forêt d'Écouves and back to Alençon.

BALLEROY, CHÂTEAU DE ✪

A long tree-lined road leads through Balleroy to this early 17th-century mansion overlooking the Drôme Valley. The symmetrical pink and grey château, built by François Mansart for Jean de Choisy, was bought in 1970 by the American publishing magnate Malcolm Forbes. His passion for ballooning inspired the Musée des Ballons that traces the sport's history from the first passenger flight in 1783 to barrage balloons of World War II.

- 🔲 50B4
- ✉ 15km southwest of Bayeux, off D572
- ☎ 02 31 21 60 61
- ⏰ Mid-Mar to mid-Oct, Wed–Mon 9–12, 2–6; Jul–Aug daily 10–6
- 🚌 From Bayeux
- 💰 Expensive

BAYEUX ✪✪✪

Bayeux's chief attraction is its tapestry (► 18), yet the town itself has great charm. An air of quiet prosperity hangs over its old stone and timber-framed buildings; the Aure river flows past watermills, and the cathedral forms a graceful focus. Built by Odo – sponsor of the tapestry – the cathedral still has its original towers and crypt. The nave's 12th-century arcades are decorated with Romanesque and oriental designs, and interesting frescos include a portrayal of Thomas à Becket's murder, while angels play musical instruments in the crypt. Beside the cathedral, the Musée Baron Gérard includes porcelain, furniture and paintings. The **Musée Mémorial de la Bataille de Normandie 1944** presents a vivid picture of the Battle of Normandy.

- 🔲 50B5
- 🍴 Choice of restaurants on rue St-Jean (€–€€€)
- 🚌 From Caen
- 🚆 Six per day from Cherbourg, 12 per day from Caen
- ↔ Caen (► 52–54), Arromanches (► 55), Cérisy-la-Forêt (► 62)

Musée Mémorial de la Bataille de Normandie 1944
- ✉ boulevard Fabian Ware
- ☎ 02 31 51 46 90
- ⏰ May to mid-Sep, 9:30–6:30; mid-Sep to Apr, 10–12:30, 2–6. Closed 25 Dec, 1 Jan, mid-Jan–1 Feb
- ♿ Very good
- 💰 Moderate

The cathedral of Bayeux; original showplace of the tapestry

BEAUMESNIL, CHÂTEAU DE ✪✪

Behind the hamlet of Beaumesnil this 17th-century red-brick and stone château appears suddenly amid formal gardens, guarded by iron gates and railings. All that remains of the medieval fortress that once stood here is the overgrown base of its donjon. The later building has fashionable Flemish designs, and the grounds were laid out by La Quintinie, a student of André Le Nôtre. The interior contains a fine library, period furniture and a museum of bookbinding.

BEAUMONT-LE-ROGER ✪

Situated on the edge of the Forêt de Beaumont, the walls of the priory ruins rise like a cliff from the roadside. Roger de Vieilles founded the Prieuré de la Sainte Trinité in 1070 near his castle, but the present remains are 13th-century. A steep path climbs under a series of arches to the hilltop ruins of the nave, with its wide eastern arch and a blind arcade along the length of the north wall. After the priory fell into disuse in the 1780s its relics were taken to the late medieval Église St-Nicolas near by.

Tour St-Nicolas, lone survivor of the great medieval abbey of le Bec-Hellouin

BEC-HELLOUIN, ABBAYE DU ✪✪

This walled Benedictine abbey in the tranquil Risle Valley was once a powerful religious, scholarly and political centre. The first two Norman archbishops of Canterbury, Lanfranc and Anselm, came from Bec; the abbey also produced many other influential churchmen, some of whom are listed on the 15th-century Tour St-Nicolas. In the new abbey church is the tomb of the anchorite Herluin who founded the community in 1034; Lanfranc arrived eight years later having abandoned his teaching at Avranches. The monks fled during the French Revolution, but in 1948 a new community was re-established here – though not before the vast abbey church had been demolished (its foundations can still be seen opposite the tower, the only part to survive).

BERNAY ☆

Bernay's 11th-century abbey was founded by Judith of Brittany, wife of Duke Richard II, and its church still dominates this substantial country town where tributaries of the Charentonne wind among the streets. The interior of the early Romanesque church has carved capitals in the choir showing animals and foliage in the style of manuscript illuminations. Cars park opposite the apse, which is strikingly decorated with wooden tiles, and the abbey gardens lead to the **Musée Municipal** in the former abbot's lodge, with its collection of art, sculpture and furniture. The town hall occupies the old abbey buildings beside the remains of the 13th-century cloisters. The Église Ste-Croix, on rue Alexandre, houses the tombstones of past abbots and of Guillaume d'Auvillars, a 15th-century abbot of le Bec-Helloüin.

BEUVRON-EN-AUGE ☆☆

Set in the heart of the Pays d'Auge, surrounded by orchards, stud farms and grazing cattle, Beuvron-en-Auge must be one of Normandy's prettiest villages. Timber-framed town houses surround the central square, where the steep-roofed *halles* (covered market) contain the Pavé d'Auge restaurant (▶ 97). At the edge of the village the Vieux Manoir, with its cross-braced timbers, is decorated with woodcarvings of faces and figures.

🚩 51E4

🍴 Restaurants, bars in town

🚌 From Pont-Audemer

🚌 Six per day from Lisieux, 5 per day from Évreux

↔ Château de Beaumesnil, Beaumont-le-Roger (▶ 58)

Musée Municipal

✉ place Guillaume de Volpiano

☎ 02 32 46 63 23

🕐 Wed–Mon 10–12, 2–5:30 (till 7 from last weekend Jun–first week Sep, and Easter hol); Sun and public hols 3–5:30

💷 Cheap

🚩 50C4

🍴 Auberge de la Boule d'Or (£–££), Pavé d'Auge (££–£££)

↔ Crèvecœur-en-Auge (▶ 63)

The Vieux Manoir, Beuvron-en-Auge

BRIONNE

Brionne's importance as a strategic town goes back to the 11th century. Duke William laid siege to it between 1047 and 1050, eventually chasing out the duke of Burgundy. On a hill overlooking the town and the Risle Valley are the massive walls of a ruined 12th-century donjon. The slate-spired Église St-Martin is mainly 15th-century.

About 7km east of Brionne, an agricultural school occupies the moated Château d'Harcourt, set in extensive parkland and originally built for Robert of Harcourt, a companion of King Richard I of England.

51E4
Restaurants and bars in town (€–€€)
From Évreux
Five per day from Rouen/Caen
Abbaye du Bec-Hellouin (▶ 58)

BROGLIE

Broglie is a small rural town in the wooded Charentonne Valley. The 18th-century château (private) looms above the town on the site of an older fortress, and timber-framed houses crowd around the 12th-century Église St-Martin, built of contrasting conglomerate and limestone with later timber additions. Behind the church is an old house whose timbers are carved with dragons and the weathered face of a green man. Plaques commemorate two of Broglie's distinguished sons: Jean-François Merimée, born here in 1757 and later secretary of the École Nationale des Beaux-Arts; and civil engineer Augustin-Jean Fresnel, famous for his work in optics, born in 1788. A garden created on the marshy riverbank near the town centre displays willows, bamboo, ornamental rhubarb and other water-loving plants.

51E4
Restaurants and bars in town
Bernay (▶ 59)

> ### Did you know ?
>
> Prince Louis-Victor (1892–1987), seventh duke of Broglie, won the Nobel Prize for physics in 1929 after discovering that electrons had wavelike properties, so helping to lay the foundation of quantum mechanics.

CABOURG

This prosperous seaside resort has retained its 19th-century air of elegance. Dominating the long but featureless promenade is the Grand Hôtel, which lives up to its name and still trades on its association with Marcel Proust; the writer stayed here and based his fictional 'Balbec' on the town (▶ 104). The beach is long and sandy, overlooked by the Grand's wide windows that recall Proust's descriptions of passers-by gazing at the rich diners in their 'aquarium'.

50C5
Choice of restaurants and bars (€–€€€)
From Caen
Three per day from Lisieux in season
Dives-sur-Mer (▶ 64)

Top right: *copper utensils in the kitchen of Carrouges*
Opposite: *enjoying the sun on Cabourg beach*

CANAPVILLE ✪

The bishops of Lisieux once resided here in the attractive timber-framed manor house set between the Touques river and the busy N177. Built between the 13th and 15th centuries, the Manoir des Évêques is set in attractive gardens and has interesting carvings – including one of a bishop's head on the gatepost.

🗺 51D5
🍴 Restaurants in village (€–€€)
🚌 From Lisieux
🔁 Deauville (▶ 64), Pont l'Évêque (▶ 72), Trouville (▶ 75)

CARROUGES, CHÂTEAU DE ✪✪

An ornate stone gatehouse with four steep-roofed towers provides the entrance to this handsome red-brick building

set in attractive parkland beyond the village of Carrouges. Until the 1930s the château was owned by the Le Veneur de Tillières family, who had lived there for nearly 500 years. The earliest part of the present building was built in the 14th century for Jean de Carrouges. Tours lead upstairs and downstairs: from the panelled Louis XI room, where the king himself stayed, to the 15th-century kitchen arrayed with pots and pans. A craft centre and the Parc Naturel Régional Normandie-Maine information centre are based in the park.

🗺 50C2
☎ 02 33 56 10 36
🕐 Apr–mid-Jun, Sep, 10–12, 2–6; mid-Jun–Aug, 9:30–12, 2–6:30; Oct–Mar, 10–12, 2–4:30. Closed 1 Jan, 1 May, 1 & 11 Nov, 25 Dec
🍴 La Boulangerie: teas and breakfasts for groups (€€).
🚌 From Argentan/Alençon
♿ Few
💰 Expensive
🔁 Argentan (▶ 55), Sées (▶ 74)

Above: *la Lande viaduct,
crossing the Orne near
Clécy*

CÉRISY-LA-FORÊT ✪

There has been a monastery in this quiet spot, on the edge of the Cérisy beech woods, since the 6th century. St Vigor established a community here about 510, and a later building was commissioned by William the Conqueror's father, Duke Robert. The present Benedictine abbey church dates from the 12th century, built in cream limestone and partly dismantled in 1812 when it proved too large for its new role of parish church. The west end of the nave has gone but the carved choir stalls in the apse have survived. Work continues to strengthen the transept where fissures have appeared; the foundations were previously reinforced in the 15th and 17th centuries. A small museum features statuary, floor tiles and other items rescued from the abbey church, and there is an exhibition of Romanesque art in lower Normandy.

CHAMP-DE-BATAILLE, CHÂTEAU DU ✪✪

This grand red-brick and stone château stands in a flat, open landscape ringed with woodland, and retains the atmosphere of an aristocratic country house. Part of the building is used as a golf club – the course is laid out within the grounds – but the main rooms are open to the public and include the duchess's bedroom, the billiard room, hung with tapestries, and a hall decorated with carvings representing the four seasons.

CLÉCY ✪

Houseboats, restaurants and bars line the Orne river on the approach to Clécy, which is centred on its 19th-century church. The main attraction of the village is its position in the Suisse Normande, surrounded by hill walks and viewpoints, one of the most popular being the Pain de Sucre that looks out across the Orne Valley. Model trains run around a miniature Suisse Normande at the Musée du Chemin de Fer Miniature (► 110).

CONCHES-EN-OUCHE ⊗

Conches lies on the edge of yet another ancient Norman territory, the Pays d'Ouche, with views of the Forêt de Conches to the west, and from the medieval château the lush Rouloir Valley to the east. The château ruins consist of a circular donjon and overgrown towers, all grouped on a motte and set in a small public garden. Near by, the Église Ste-Foy has an elaborate iron spire and carved 16th-century door. Both fortress and church are associated with the lords of Tosny: the former was built by them in the 12th century and the latter occupies the site of a church founded by Roger de Tosny in the 11th century, who returned from a pilgrimage bearing relics of Sainte Foy.

CRÈVECŒUR-EN-AUGE ⊗⊗

An attractive cluster of traditional timber-framed and stone buildings represent the château founded here in the 11th century. Within the moated complex are remains of the donjon and its enclosure, and the chapel and workshops eventually taken over as farm buildings. These have been restored by the present owners, the Schlumberger Foundation, whose work in the oil industry is covered in an exhibition next door to the site.

🕀 51F3
🍴 Choice of restaurants (€–€€)
🚌 From Évreux
🚂 Five per day from Évreux
↔ Évreux (► 65)

🕀 51D4
☎ 02 31 63 02 45
🕐 Apr–Sep, daily 11–6 (Jul–Aug 11–7), Sun, Oct 2–6. Closed Tue in Apr, May, Jun, Sep
🍴 Auberge du Cheval Blanc (€€)
🚌 From Lisieux during school terms
♿ Few
✋ Moderate
↔ Beuvron-en-Auge (► 59), Lisieux (► 66)

The 15th- to 16th-century gatehouse of the Château de Crèvecœur

63

Above: *racing for the Grand Prix, Deauville*

DEAUVILLE ✪✪

Two Côte Fleurie resorts, Deauville and Trouville, face each other across the Touques river – but it is Deauville that attracts the moneyed tourist. Eugène Cornuché built the racecourse, casino and les Planches, a long seafront boardwalk, in 1910, and each summer the big spenders continue to arrive; beach huts boast the names of celebrities past and present. From July to the end of August events include the American Film Festival, the Grand Prix horse race and a tennis tournament; out of season the town hibernates.

DIVES-SUR-MER ✪

Duke William embarked from this former inland port to conquer England, and later had a church built here, Notre-Dame, much restored and rebuilt since. Near by are the town's wooden *halles* (covered markets), built in the 15th century so that the local monastery could collect market duties. Craft shops and a restaurant have been set up near the yachting marina in a 16th-century inn, now known as the Village Guillaume-le-Conquérant.

DOMFRONT ✪✪

Old and new Domfront sprawl from the ruined hilltop fortress high above the Varenne river. In the upper quarter, stone and timber-framed houses seem to grow from the ramparts and towers, and huddle for safety over narrow cobbled streets. The fortress was built in 1092 by the son of William the Conqueror, later King Henry I of England. On the riverside at the bottom of the hill is the 11th- to 12th-century Église Notre-Dame-sur-l'Eau, where Thomas à Becket is said to have celebrated mass in 1166.

ÉVREUX ✪✪

The ancient capital of Eure, on the banks of the Iton, has been rebuilt many times following invasion, siege and war, yet still preserves some notable historic monuments and an attractive centre. A riverside walk leads from the restored 12th- to 17th-century Cathédrale Notre-Dame to the Tour de l'Horloge, a free-standing tower built in 1490. The tower's bell strikes the hour.

Évreux's turbulent history is traced in the Musée de l'Ancien Évêché next to the cathedral, housed in the former 15th-century bishop's palace. Grouped around the central place Charles de Gaulle are the elegant 19th-century Hôtel Dieu, Maison des Arts, theatre, and the library with its startling modern annexe in the form of a wooden bowl. West of the centre lies the 12th-century Église St-Taurin; the one-time abbey church contains a fine 13th-century reliquary, gold-plated with enamelled silver, that contains the relics of Saint Taurin.

FALAISE ✪✪✪

William the Conqueror's birthplace has become the subject of fierce controversy. It was at Falaise that his father, Robert, took a fancy to Arlette, a tanner's daughter, as she washed her clothes in the river; rejecting all secrecy, she later met Robert inside the **château** and subsequently gave birth to William there. The modern controversy concerns the restoration of the site's 12th-century donjon, its chapel, and the 13th-century Tour de Talbot. Bruno Decaris's concrete and steel additions have shocked traditionalists, but their sudden plunging views and glimpses of thick stonework give a sense of the former military might often missing at similar monuments. A glass floor reveals the foundations of Duke Robert's stronghold, and delicately carved windows can be seen behind etched reinforced glass. A walk around the top of the Tour de Talbot offers dizzy views over the Ante Valley.

🚩 51F4
🍴 Choice of restaurants (€–€€€)
🚌 From Rouen and Honfleur
🚆 Five per day from Cherbourg
↔ Conches-en-Ouche (► 63)

🚩 50C3
🍴 La Fine Fourchette, rue G Clemenceau (€–€€)
🚌 From Caen
↔ Château de Vendeuvre (► 75)

Château
☎ 02 31 41 61 44
🕐 Daily mid-Feb–Jun, Sep–Dec, 10–6; Jul, Aug, 10–7. Closed Tue, Wed, Oct–Mar
♿ None
💷 Moderate
❓ Guided tours every hour; English tour 1:30

Above: *ornate craftsmanship on a fountain at Évreux*

Left: *the mighty château at Falaise towers above the Ante river*

50B5

📞 02 31 80 00 42

🕐 Easter–mid-Jun, mid-Sep–Oct, Sat, Sun, hols, 2:30–6:30; Wed–Mon, mid-Jun–mid-Sep, 2:30–6:30

🍴 Restaurant at Basly, northeast, and in village (€€)

🚌 From Caen

💶 Expensive

↔ Caen (▶ 52–54)

FONTAINE-HENRY, CHÂTEAU DE ✪✪✪

As the D141 follows the Mue river towards Fontaine-Henry, the château can be glimpsed among the trees across the valley; but only when the road has climbed through the quiet Caen-stone hamlet is the building's extraordinary façade revealed. The earliest part, built in the 1490s for the Harcourt family, is a stone wing decorated with elegant carvings. The later wing, added in about 1550, is completely different: top-heavy with precipitous slate roofs that rise as high as the main walls below. Still privately owned, the château houses a collection of 17th- to 18th-century French paintings, and there is a late medieval chapel in the grounds.

51D4

🍴 Choice of restaurants (€–€€€)

🚌 From Rouen

🚆 Five per day from Rouen, 10 per day from Évreux (Paris–Dives line)

↔ Beuvron-en-Auge (▶ 59), Crèvecœur-en-Auge (▶ 63), Pont-l'Évêque (▶ 72), St-Germain-de-Livet (▶ 72)

Les Buissonnets

✉ 22 Chemin des Buissonnets

📞 02 31 48 55 08

🕐 Easter–end Sep, daily 9–12, 2–6 (May and Jun 5:30); Oct–Nov, 10–12, 2–5; Dec and Feb–Easter, 10–12, 2–4. Closed Jan

♿ Few 💶 Free

LISIEUX ✪

Pilgrims come in thousands to Lisieux, the town where Sainte Thérèse lived as a child (▶ 67, panel). It is also the main centre of the Pays d'Auge. Apart from a scatter of old houses near the 13th-century cathedral and the Hôtel de Ville, the centre is largely modern and nondescript; the main interest lies in the places associated with Thérèse, including **les Buissonnets** where she lived as a girl. The massive, domed Basilique Ste-Thérèse, consecrated in the 1950s, stands out among concrete and glass office blocks; its 45m belfry houses no fewer than 44 bells, and an exhibition describes the life led by Thérèse and other Carmelite nuns. The saint's relics are kept in the Chapelle du Carmel, guarded by a statue of the Virgin that was once owned by her family.

Left: a statue of Sainte Thérèse, near les Buissonnets

Left: *a lavishly furnished bedroom in the Château de Fontaine-Henry*
Below: *the rooftops and greenery of Mortagne-au-Perche, once a regional capital, now a peaceful country town*

MORTAGNE-AU-PERCHE ✪✪

Former capital of the Perche, Mortagne stands on a hill overlooking a gentle landscape of meadows, red-roofed farms and wooded hills. Dilapidated houses with wrought-iron balconies line the streets, and the only remaining fortification, the Porte St-Denis, houses a regional museum, the Musée Percheron. The 15th-century Église Notre-Dame has good woodwork around the altar.

🚩 51E2
🍴 Choice of restaurants (€–€€)
🚌 From Alençon
↔ Alençon (➤ 55), Sées (➤ 74)

O, CHÂTEAU D' (➤ 20, TOP TEN)

ORBEC ✪✪

This unassuming market town has a good collection of crooked timber-framed houses, including the 16th-century Vieux Manoir that houses the **Musée Municipal**, whose collection of paintings, ceramics and other artefacts recall the history and traditions of the Pays d'Auge. The Église Notre-Dame has a massive belfry, originally a defensive tower in the 15th century but given a more decorative finish in the following century.

🚩 51E4
🍴 Restaurants in town (€–€€€)
🚌 From Lisieux

Musée Municipal
✉ Grande Rue
☎ 02 31 32 58 89
🕐 Jul, Aug, Wed, Sat, Sun, 10–12, 2–6, Mon, Thu, Fri 2–6; Easter–Jun, Sep–Dec, Wed, Sat, Sun, 2–6
♿ None
🎟 Free
↔ Broglie (➤ 60), Lisieux (➤ 66)

Did you know ?

Sainte Thérèse was born Thérèse Martin in 1873. At the age of nine she begged her father to let her enter the Carmelite convent with her sister; she was admitted at 15, but died of tuberculosis at 24. Her pious memoirs, History of a Soul, *were published posthumously, reaching a wide and enthusiastic readership. Thérèse was canonised in 1925 for her intense piety and devotion.*

In the Know

If you only have a short time to visit Normandy, or would like to get a real flavour of the region, here are some ideas:

10
Ways to Be a Local

Try your French – even a stumbling attempt will be much appreciated.

Relax in a café or brasserie with a coffee and a newspaper and let the world go by.

Forget about lunchtime shopping – many town and village shops in Normandy shut between 12 and 2 (but remain open long after office hours).

Visit an Algerian or Moroccan restaurant and try the cheap and tasty couscous or *tadjine* dishes.

Remember the courtesies of a language that still adheres to formality: always greet others with a *bonjour Madame* or *Monsieur*, take your leave with *au revoir* and the appropriate title.

Treat mealtimes as social occasions, a time for lively debate and discussion, not just for refuelling.

Use public transport – it's clean, efficient, and a great way to see the countryside.

See a film – the Normans (like the rest of France) are dedicated cinemagoers.

Learn to play *boules* – or, if that seems too daunting a task, linger to watch a quiet match in almost any village or corner of town.

Eat meat – or at least be prepared for the fact that vegetarian dishes are rarely even a token item on most restaurant menus.

10
Good Places to Have Lunch

Auberge de Goury (€–€€)
✉ Goury, Cap de la Hague
☎ 02 33 52 77 01. At the tip of the Cotentin peninsula, opposite a lifeboat station and lighthouse. Grills, seafood; closed Sunday evening and Monday evening.

Auberge St-Maclou (€–€€)
✉ 224 rue Martainville, Rouen ☎ 02 35 71 06 67. Particularly good-value set menus at lunchtime in an old Rouen building near Église St-Maclou.

Camomille (€€)
✉ 23 rue de Grenoble, Évreux ☎ 02 32 38 30 90. Generous omelettes and salads, and a good range of teas and pastries.

La Marine (€–€€)
✉ 146 boulevard Fernand-Moureaux, Trouville
☎ 02 31 88 12 51. Fresh seafood in a traditional restaurant overlooking the fish market and river.

Le Pavé d'Auge (€€–€€€)
✉ place du Village, Beuvron-en-Auge ☎ 02 31 79 26 71. Norman dishes in the old market hall.

La Régence (€€)
✉ 42 quai de Caligny, Cherbourg ☎ 02 33 43 05 16. Popular seafood restaurant (part of the Hôtel Régence), with good views of the harbour and fishing boats.

Les Roches Blanches (€€)
✉ front de la mer, Étretat
☎ 02 35 27 07 34. Seafood with a fine sea view in a long building tucked under the cliff.

La Taverne de Maître Kanter (€€) ✉ 1 avenue du 6 Juin, Caen ☎ 02 31 50 02 22. Brasserie serving salads, grills, sauerkrauts and seafood. Open midday to midnight.

Les Terrasses Poulard (€–€€) ✉ 18 Grande Rue, le Mont-St-Michel ☎ 02 33 60 14 09. Omelettes and seafood on the mount, with spectacular bay views.

Le Vieux Honfleur (€€–€€€) ✉ 13 quai St-Étienne, Honfleur ☎ 02 31 89 15 31. Outdoor tables overlooking the harbour, with especially fine seafood.

Good fare and lively conversation in the resort of Honfleur

10
Top Activities

Canoeing on the Suisse Normande rivers, particularly the fast-flowing Orne.

Cycling along the Seine Valley, the Eure Valley and the Côte d'Albâtre; also in the forests of Brotonne and Lyons (➤ 115).

Fishing – sea fishing from resorts along the coast; also inland on lakes and rivers (➤ 114). Membership of angling associations and details of permits available at each *département* tourist office (➤ 120).

Golf – 27-hole courses open to amateurs at Deauville, Étretat and Granville; 18-hole courses at Cabourg, Caen, Clécy, Houlgate, Deauville, Dieppe, Évreux, Le Havre and Rouen (two); nine-hole courses at Bagnoles and Cherbourg (➤ 114).

Horse racing – courses at Alençon, Argentan, Caen, Deauville, Lisieux and Rouen, among many others.

Horse riding – treks and rides organised by centres throughout the region; along the shores of Calvados and Manche, and through woodlands and countryside in Eure and Orne (➤ 115).

Thalassotherapy (sea-water therapy) along the Côte Fleurie, especially in Deauville, Luc-sur-Mer, Ouistreham and Trouville; also Dieppe and Granville.

Walking on footpaths along the Seine, between Étretat and le Tréport, and across the Parc Naturel Régional Normandie-Maine and the Cotentin peninsula. There are also steeper hikes in the Suisse Normande.

Windsurfing – good, long beaches on the coastline of Calvados and western Manche.

Yachting – marinas or moorings at Barfleur, Barneville-Carteret, Cabourg, Deauville, Dieppe, Granville, Fécamp, Le Havre, Honfleur, Ouistreham, St-Valéry-en-Caux, and le Tréport.

10
Top Views

- Seine Valley, from Château Gaillard (➤ 17).
- Rouvre Valley and Suisse Normande, from Roche d'Oëtre (➤ 72).
- Bay of le Mont-St-Michel, from the abbey (➤ 24–25).
- Vire Valley, from the Roches de Ham (➤ 90).
- The Baie d'Écalgrain and towards the Channel Islands, from Nez de

Children learning to sail at Le Havre

Jobourg (➤ 82).
- Côte de Nacre, from the Pointe du Hoc (➤ 70).
- Côte d'Albâtre, from the Falaise d'Amont (➤ 39).
- Orne Valley, from Pain de Sucre, near Clécy (➤ 62).
- Hilltop spires of Coutances, on the northern approach (➤ 84).
- Remains of Abbaye de Hambye, in the Sienne Valley (➤ 85).

5
Conqueror Connections

- **Barfleur:** Duke William's flagship, *Mora*, shown on the Bayeux Tapestry, was built here.
- **Bayeux:** William's half-brother, Bishop Odo, completed the cathedral and commissioned the tapestry depicting William's victory at Hastings (➤ 18).
- **Caen:** William founded the two abbeys as mausoleums for himself and his wife (➤ 52).
- **Dives-sur-Mer:** William gathered his fleet and army here, prior to the invasion of England (➤ 64).
- **Falaise:** birthplace of William in 1027 (➤ 65).

✚ 50C5
🍴 Choice of cafés and
restaurants near ferry
terminal and beach
(€–€€€)
🚌 From Caen
↔ Caen (▶ 52–54), Cabourg
(▶ 60)

✚ 51D3
☎ 02 33 36 68 68
🕐 Guided tour: Apr–mid-
Oct, daily 9:30–6; mid-
Oct–Mar, daily 2–5
🍴 Restaurant near by (€€)
🚌 From Argentan to
Nonant-le-Pin
🔽 Moderate

✚ 50A5
🍴 Choice of restaurants at
Grandcamp-Maisy
🚌 From Bayeux to
Grandcamp-Maisy

*One of the famous
Percheron horses is put
through its paces at le
Pin-au-Haras*

OUISTREHAM ✪

The ferry port of Ouistreham also offers a cheerful yacht marina and the beach resort of Riva-Bella. Set back from the coast, among suburban villas, are reminders of D-Day's Sword Beach: the Musée du Mur de l'Atlantique housed in the German range-finding station, Big Bunker; and the Musée du Débarquement No 4 Commando, opposite the casino, with military exhibits from World War II.

PIN-AU-HARAS, LE ✪✪

Louis XIV's minister Colbert set up the national stud in 1665, but it was abolished briefly during the Revolution. Re-established in the 19th century, its breeds include Percherons, Norman cobs and English thoroughbreds. Beyond the wrought-iron gate, topped with a gold horse's head, staff live and work in the 18th-century château, with the stable wings on either side. Walks and rides lead off into woodland, and the gentle Pays d'Auge landscape stretches into the distance.

POINTE DU HOC ✪✪✪

Nothing evokes the scale and violence of the 1944 landings more poignantly than this 30m clifftop position overlooking Omaha Beach. This German observation point was heavily bombarded, thus allowing American Rangers to climb the sheer rocks, albeit with heavy casualties; their story is told in the Musée des Rangers at Grandcamp-Maisy, 5km west. A viewing platform and memorial have been set up on the headland, a surreal landscape of modern megaliths: massive slabs of concrete lie scattered amid vast craters, now softened by grass. From the platform there are clear views of the invasion coast and the site itself, now silent except for the call of seagulls.

A Drive Along the D-Day Beaches

From Caen take the D514 towards Ouistreham.

A short detour (follow signs) leads to Pegasus Bridge, captured by British parachutists on 5 June 1944. Sound-and-light shows take place between April and October.

From Ouistreham (▶ 70) and Sword Beach, continue through St-Aubin and Courseulles (Juno Beach) to Arromanches (▶ 55).

Between Courseulles (with its colourful art-deco casino) and Arromanches, the flat marshes of the Gold Beach area offer wide sea views.

Follow the D514 from Arromanches and turn left on to the D127, joining the D87 before Ryes.

Continue through the village on the D87 to visit the British and Commonwealth cemetery.

From the cemetery return to the D112 and turn left, following signs to Sommervieu. Join the D12 into Bayeux (▶ 57). The D6 goes north to Port-en-Bessin and the Musée des Épaves sous-marines du Débarquement (Museum of Underwater Wrecks of the [D-Day] Landings). Follow the D514 along Omaha Beach.

At Colleville-sur-Mer, follow signs for the American cemetery, one of two war cemeteries for US troops.

Return to the D514 and continue west to Pointe du Hoc (▶ 70). Return to the D514 and turn right, continuing to Grandcamp–Maisy and the Musée des Rangers. The D199 goes south and joins the D113 (left) and D613 (left) for la Cambe and the German cemetery.

To continue to Utah Beach, take the N13 west, then the D913 to Ste-Marie-du-Mont, then drive to the coast.

Distance
80km to la Cambe; a further 28km to Utah Beach

Time
3½ hours to la Cambe without stops

Start point
Caen
✚ 50C4

End point
La Cambe
✚ 50A5

Lunch
Le Lion d'Or (€€)
✉ 71 rue St-Jean, Bayeux
☎ 02 31 22 15 64

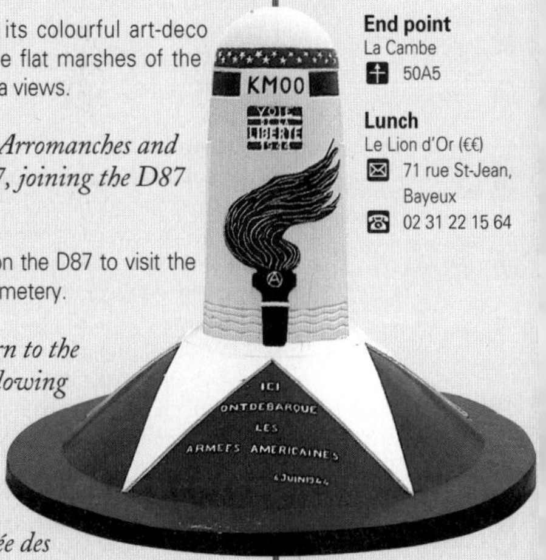

The first D-Day milestone, a 'Liberty Way' marker, at la Madeleine, near Utah Beach

51D5
Choice of restaurants (€–€€€)
From Lisieux

Musée du Calvados et des Métiers Anciens
Distillerie du Père Magloire, route de Deauville
02 31 64 30 31
Easter–Oct, 10–12:30, 2:30–6:30
Cheap

50C3
Restaurant and bars at Pont-d'Ouilly (€–€€)
From Caen to Clécy
Clécy (▶ 62)

Below: *the extraordinary moated château at St-Germain-de-Livet*

51D4
02 31 31 00 03
Feb–Nov, 11–6. Closed Dec, Jan and first 2 weeks in Nov
Restaurants at Lisieux (€–€€€)
53 from Lisieux
Few
Moderate
Lisieux (▶ 66)

PONT-L'ÉVÊQUE ✪

Cheese is the principal claim to fame of this historic town in the Touques Valley. Its soft and creamy speciality was first produced in the 12th century, when the town was known as Angelot; it only took the name of Pont-l'Évêque some 500 years later. Attractive timber-framed buildings survive, as well as the Flamboyant Église St-Michel where plaques commemorate the victims of the Franco-Prussian War and other conflicts. The **Musée du Calvados et des Métiers Anciens** describes traditional methods of making calvados. In the nearby Château de Bettevillethe, the Musée de la Belle Époque de l'Automobile has a collection of vintage vehicles (1800–1960s).

ROCHE D'OËTRE ✪✪

A track leads from the roadside to this 118m rocky precipice that offers some of the best views of the Suisse Normande's wooded slopes. A viewing table points out the main landmarks (take care – there's nothing between you and the drop): the panorama extends over the Orne Valley and the Rouvre gorges, and southeast towards the Lac du Rabodanges.

The small town of Pont-d'Ouilly, downriver, is a good centre for exploring the area, and has pleasant walks alongside the fast-flowing Orne.

ST-GERMAIN-DE-LIVET ✪✪✪

Hidden in the dip of an isolated tributary of the Touques is a château straight from a children's picture book. The two surviving wings join at the ornate gatehouse: a 15th-century timber-framed range and a turreted 16th-century wing, its ostentatious chequered walls built using limestone, and green-glazed and red bricks. Frescos are preserved in the older house, while the later wing has a gallery of 19th-century paintings and a room decorated with terracotta tiles. The decorative style

of brickwork found on the chateau can be seen also in the transept of the church opposite.

ST-PIERRE-SUR-DIVES ✪✪

On Monday mornings this small country town bursts into life as the market sets up in the cavernous, barn-like *halles*. Inside, the beamed roof echoes with the cacophony of ducks, turkeys, chickens and stall-holders, and the gabble continues at the brick stalls outside. Originally built in the 11th century, the hall was faithfully rebuilt after World War II using 290,000 wooden dowels and not a single nail. In the town's large church, once part of a Benedictine abbey, the 'Meridian', a line carved across the nave, flanked by signs of the zodiac and almost worn away in parts, indicates the position of the sun at noon.

SASSY, CHÂTEAU DE ✪

Beyond the hamlet of St-Christophe-le-Jajolet, on the brow of a wooded hill, this 18th-century red-brick château overlooks its terraced garden. It was begun in 1760 and passed in 1850 to the dukes of Audriffet-Pasquier, the current owners. Items on display include tapestries and a lock of hair cut from Louis XVI's head; the doomed king presented it to a member of the Pasquier family who had acted as his defence counsel.

Antiques on sale in the St-Pierre halles

➕ 51D4
🍴 Restaurants, cafés (€–€€)
🚌 From Lisieux (during school terms)
↔ Château de Vendeuvre (▶ 75)

Les Halles
🕐 Apr–Oct 8–8; otherwise apply to tourist office
♿ Few
❓ Antiques market first Mon of every month

➕ 50C2
☎ 02 33 35 32 66
🕐 Easter–Oct, daily 3–6; grounds all year daily
🍴 None
🚌 From Alençon to St-Christophe-le-Jajolet
 Moderate

73

Above and right: *life on the beach and boardwalk at Trouville*

⊞ 51D2
🍴 Choice of restaurants and cafés (€–€€€)
🚌 From Alençon
🚆 Three per day from Rouen
↔ Château d'O (► 20)

Musée Départemental d'Art Religieux
✉ 7 place du Général-de-Gaulle
☎ 02 33 81 23 00
🕐 Jul–Sep, Wed–Mon 10–6
💷 Cheap

⊞ 50B4
🍴 Choice of restaurants near river (€€–€€€)
🚌 From Caen
↔ Caen (► 52–54), Clécy (► 62)

SÉES ✪✪

Sées, close to the source of the Orne on whose banks the town stands, has been an important religious centre since AD 400, when Saint Latuin became its first bishop. The town is dominated by its splendid Gothic cathedral, the classical bishop's palace, and the former canons' lodgings that now house the **Musée Départemental d'Art Religieux**. The western façade of the cathedral was bolstered with buttresses in the 16th century when it began to lean dangerously. Dramatic 13th-century stained-glass windows light the transept, and delicate tracery decorates the nave arcades and windows. In the porch, faded carvings can still be made out, including a cat carrying its kitten, and a double-headed eagle.

THURY-HARCOURT ✪

This pleasant Suisse Normande centre, beside the Orne river, acquired its name from two sources: 'Thury', according to local legend, from a Viking cry, *Thor Aïe*; and Harcourt from the eponymous family who lived in the 11th-century château. Much of the former fortress was destroyed during World War II and only the skeletal façade remains, surrounded by restored gardens and a park.

TROUVILLE-SUR-MER ★★

Deauville's neighbour across the Touques estuary, Trouville is the more appealing and cheerful of the two resorts, with its fishing boats, the tree-lined boulevard Fernand Moureaux, and a wide sandy beach and boardwalk. Garish lights advertise the Louisiana Follies at the salmon-pink casino, and fish, reptiles and insects are on display at the Aquarium Écologique. Set back from the seafront, the Église Notre-Dame de Bon-Secours has intricate stained-glass windows and an ornate 19th-century façade, and the Musée Villa Montebello houses paintings by Eugène Boudin; the museum also traces the history of sea bathing that became the rage here in the 1820s.

🔳 51D5
🍴 Choice of restaurants along boulevard Fernand Moureaux and rue Carnot (€–€€)
🚆 From Lisieux and Caen
🚌 Eight per day from Lisieux
↔️ Canapville (▶ 61), Deauville (▶ 64)

VENDEUVRE, CHÂTEAU DE ★★

Set among formal flower beds and an ornamental water garden, this 18th-century château houses some intriguing curiosities, including a chair designed for fashion-conscious women in panniers (the 'saddlebags' worn to widen skirts). The main attraction, though, is the Musée de Mobilier Miniature, a collection of tiny masterpieces made from the 16th century to the present day. These include silverware, embroidery, furniture and cutlery, all in immaculate, scaled-down detail; one of the most popular items is a miniature bed, complete with hangings, made in the 18th century for the pet cat of Louis XV's daughter.

🔳 50C4
☎️ 02 31 40 93 83
🕐 May, Jun, Sep, 11–6; Jul, Aug, 11–6:30; Apr, Oct–mid-Nov, Sun, school hols, 2–6
🍴 Tea room (€€)
♿ Few
💰 Expensive
↔️ Falaise (▶ 65), St-Pierre-sur-Dives (▶ 73)

VERNEUIL-SUR-AVRE ★

Historic Verneuil is composed of three precincts. Each was once protected by a series of moated walls, and you can still walk along part of the outer moat that enclosed the whole town. The grim, windowless Tour Grise was built by Philippe Auguste after the French had taken the town in 1204, a circular donjon similar to the Tour Jeanne d'Arc in Rouen (▶ 35). The town suffered further during the Hundred Years War due to its position on the border between French and English territory. Timber-framed and stone buildings crowd around the Église de la Madeleine, a 12th-century church whose later, Flamboyant tower is crowned with an elegant filigree lantern. The Église Notre-Dame has 16th-century statuary by local sculptors.

🔳 51F3
🍴 Restaurants and bars in town (€–€€€)
🚆 From Évreux

The richly carved late 15th-century tower of la Madeleine, Verneuil-sur-Avre

Food & Drink

Weight-watchers are in for a tough time in Normandy. Rich dairy ingredients, mountains of fresh seafood, and local cider are just some of the temptations in store.

Pommeau
Given the abundance of local orchards it's not surprising that apples appear so frequently – on meat, in puddings and in drinks. *Pommeau* is yet another ingenious way of using the fruit: a combination of two parts apple juice and one part calvados, chilled and served as an aperitif. It can also be used, with added spices, as an ingredient in savoury dishes.

Dairy Products

Normandy boasts some of the country's most delicious and best-known cheeses. Pont-l'Évêque, a soft and creamy cheese, is made with fresh warm milk and sold in squares. The stronger and smellier Livarot, made from staler milk, is round and banded with 'stripes' that earn it the nickname 'le colonel'. Neufchâtel is a cream cheese packaged in a variety of shapes and edible after 12 days (but better after several months). Heading the bill, though, is Camembert, now made in thousands of different versions in many corners of Europe. Normandy Camembert is the genuine article: the very best bears the letters VCN (*véritable Camembert de Normandie*). Because of the wealth of dairy farms, Normans have a passion for cream and butter, particularly in the rural Pays d'Auge where almost any dish – fish, meat, potatoes or vegetables – can be served with a dairy sauce *à la vallée d'Auge*.

A variety of Camemberts – but only Normandy's version is the real thing

Seafood

Some of the freshest and tastiest seafood you will ever sample is served up in the harbourside restaurants of the coastal resorts. The list is mouthwatering: lobsters, mussels, oysters, crabs, and a multitude of fish. *Marmite dieppoise* combines the best of all worlds: a spicy stew with shrimp, mussels and white fish; for an even more impressive concoction order an *assiette de fruits de mer*, a mixture of mussels, oysters, clams, cockles, crabs and more. The pick of the seafood eateries can be found along the quays of Dieppe, Honfleur and Granville.

Meat and Offal

Squeamish carnivores would do well to avoid asking too many questions about the local menus – especially in Rouen, where the main ingredient of *canard* (duck) *rouennais* is put through all sorts of agonies for the gourmet's benefit. In order to keep the full flavour of its blood, the unfortunate bird is either strangled or smothered; alternatively it is squeezed through a press so that the juice of its bones gives an added edge to the sauce. Thus vegetarianism is a lonely occupation in a region where menus include Mortagne-au-Perche's famous *boudin noir* (black pudding), Vire's *andouilles* (chitterlings), and *tripes à la mode de Caen*, which is served after stewing for several hours.

L'Andouille de Vire
Vire chitterlings have been a local speciality since the 18th century. The sausages, made from the pig's digestive system, are smoked for six to eight weeks before being steeped and cooked in water for three or four hours. Two factors apparently account for the success of Vire's *andouille*: the cleanliness of the offal, and the long smoking process that gives it a particularly robust flavour.

Desserts and Drinks

Apples and pears feature prominently in Norman puddings, as well as in the most celebrated drinks, cider and calvados. Calvados, named after the *département*, is a brandy made from fermented and distilled apples matured in oak for up to 10 years. The *trou* (hole) *normand* is the custom of knocking back a small glass of calvados in the middle of a meal to stimulate the digestion. (Nowadays it's more likely to be a calvados and apple sorbet.) Perry, or *poiré*, is made from pears in the same way cider is produced from apples.

Popular desserts are *douillon* (pear baked in pastry) and *bouillon* (a kind of apple dumpling).

Above and below:
making the best of apples and pears in tarte Normande; Pommeau, poiré *and cider*

The Northwest

As you cross the border into Manche and travel towards the head of the Cotentin (Cherbourg) peninsula, the landscape changes and the population dwindles. At the base of the Cotentin are the fields and orchards of the *bocage*, criss-crossed with dense hedges. Empty beaches and sand dunes line the western coast, and at the tip of the peninsula waves crash against wild, granite cliffs. Cherbourg is the biggest centre, with its constant stream of ferry passengers and busy port, but the most memorable sight in the northwest – indeed in the whole of Normandy – is le Mont-St-Michel (▶ 24–25), perched upon the quicksands in the crook between Normandy and Brittany.

> '*Mont–St–Michel, said Victor Hugo, is to France what the pyramids are to Egypt. This does not describe it; but then it is indescribable …*'
>
> PERCY DEARMER
> *Highways and Byways in Normandy*
> (1900)

———————●———————

Opposite: *memories of le Mont-St-Michel*

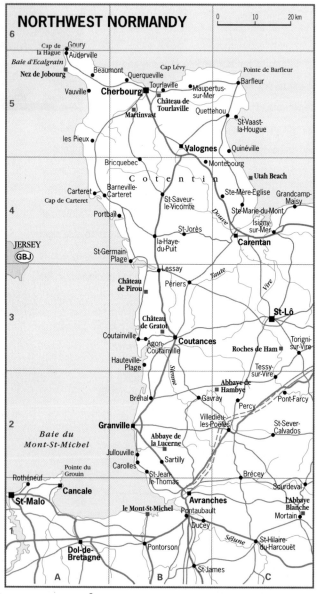

NORTHWEST NORMANDY

0   10   20 km

6

Cap de la Hague • Goury
Auderville •
Baie d'Ecalgrain
Nez de Jobourg
Beaumont •
Querqueville •
Cap Lévy
Pointe de Barfleur
Vauville •
Cherbourg
Tourlaville •
Maupertus-sur-Mer
Barfleur •

5

Château de Tourlaville
Quettehou •
Martinvast
St-Vaast-la-Hougue •
les Pieux •
Valognes
Quinéville •
Bricquebec •
Montebourg •
C o t e n t i n
Utah Beach

4

Barneville-Carteret •
Carteret •
St-Sauveur-le-Vicomte •
Ste-Mère-Église •
Grandcamp-Maisy
Cap de Carteret
Douve
Ste-Marie-du-Mont •
Portbail •
St-Jorès •
Isigny-sur-Mer •
la-Haye-du-Puit •
CARENTAN

JERSEY
(**GBJ**)

St-Germain-Plage •
Lessay •
Taute
Vire
Château de Pirou
Périers •

3

St-Lô
Château de Gratot
Coutainville •
Agon-Coutainville •
Coutances
Torigni-sur-Vire •
Hauteville-Plage •
Sienne
Roches de Ham
Tessy-sur-Vire •
Abbaye de Hambye
Bréhal •
Gavray •
Percy •
Pont-Farcy •

2

Villedieu-les-Poêles •
St-Sever-Calvados •
Granville
Baie du Mont-St-Michel
Abbaye de la Lucerne
Jullouville •
Sartilly •
Carolles •
St-Jean-le-Thomas •
Brécey •
Rothéneuf •
Pointe du Grouin
Sourdeval •
Cancale
Avranches
l'Abbaye Blanche
St-Malo
le Mont-St-Michel •
Pontaubault •
Mortain •

1

Ducey •
Sélune
Dol-de-Bretagne
Pontorson •
St-Hilaire-du-Harcouët •
St-James •

A   **B**   **C**

What to See in the Northwest

AVRANCHES ✪✪

The hilltop town above the Sée river looks out across the estuary to the church of le Mont-St-Michel, originally founded in the 8th century by Bishop Aubert of Avranches after Saint Michael had appeared to him in a vision. **Les Manuscrits du Mont-St-Michel** in the Hôtel de Ville are a collection of illuminated manuscripts associated with the famous abbey, including some fine Romanesque drawings. Behind the building are remains of an 11th-century château; steps climb to the donjon and terraced garden, with views inland and over the coast. The 19th-century Église de Notre-Dame-des-Champs is one of three churches built after the old cathedral collapsed in 1790.

BARFLEUR ✪✪

Fishing boats chug in and out, and fishermen mend their nets on the harbourside of this small granite town on the Cotentin's northeast tip. It was near here that William 'Atheling', son of King Henry I, was drowned when the White Ship sank in 1120 – an event that later led to a civil war over the English crown. A narrow passageway runs from the harbour past the 17th-century church to a beach and Normandy's tallest lighthouse (71m).

80B1

🍴 Choice of restaurants (€–€€)

🚌 From Cherbourg and Granville

🚂 Two per day from Caen

Les Manuscrits du Mont-St-Michel

☎ 02 33 89 29 40

🕐 Jul–Aug, daily 10–6; Jun–Sep, daily 10–12, 2–6

♿ Cheap

➕ 80C5

🍴 Some cafés and bars in town (€–€€)

🚌 From Cherbourg

🔄 St-Vaast-la-Hougue (► 88)

Barfleur, a traditional fishing town

BARNEVILLE-CARTERET ✪

Barneville-Carteret is a union of two different towns and their beaches. Carteret is the busier resort, with a yachting marina, and a broad sandy beach overlooked by caravans and large faded villas. Ferries travel from the harbour to Jersey and Guernsey.

Barneville, 2km away, has an austere 11th-century church with a fortified tower added later. Barneville-Plage, a long, empty stretch of sand, is reached across a cob over the Gerfleur estuary.

➕ 80A4

🍴 Restaurants in Barneville and by Carteret beach (€–€€€)

🚌 From Cherbourg

🔄 Bricquebec (► 82)

BRICQUEBEC

The impressive ruins of a 14th-century château form the focus of this small market town, whose main street runs right up to the gatehouse. Inside, the 11-sided donjon is the most prominent of a group of buildings around a pleasant courtyard; one side is taken up with the older Knights' Hall, now the Hôtel du Vieux Château. A walk along the sentry wall leads to the clock tower that houses a collection of traditional Norman furniture.

CAP DE LA HAGUE ✪✪✪

Heading west from Cherbourg, the road to the north-western finger of the Cotentin passes the vast, glittering pile of the Usine de Retraitement des Combustibles Nucléaires (nuclear fuel reprocessing centre), then turns left, between high hedges and through the narrow, dark-stone village of Dannery, for the wild rocky headland at Nez de Jobourg. A track leads past an isolated *auberge* to a viewpoint that looks across the coastline and green fields (marred only by the nuclear plant in the distance), and out to sea towards the Channel Islands. From Dannery the road winds north through a green valley to emerge at the Baie d'Écalgrain, a lovely sweep of coast sheltered by low hills. Beyond the village of Auderville the road comes to an end at Goury, a tiny harbour with a lighthouse and hexagonal lifeboat station; here you can enjoy a meal and watch the waves from the quayside.

CAROLLES ✪

Carolles is a quiet coastal village with an unassuming beach resort, set between the bustling holiday centre of Granville and Avranches. The location is its main appeal: walks lead from the centre through wooded countryside

Beach huts add colour to the resort of Carolles

Work and play – fishing boats and yachts share part of the busy harbour at Cherbourg

and along the Vallée du Lude to a remote bay. Carolles-Plage, a stretch of sand backed with beach huts and snack bars, looks north along the spectacular coastline as far as Granville. A viewpoint to the northwest, le Pignon Butor, takes in the Baie du Mont-St-Michel between Granville and the Breton headland of Pointe du Grouin.

CHERBOURG ✪✪✪

Ships have docked here since the 17th century when Vauban built the original port, and today a constant stream of ferries sail to and from England and Ireland. The art deco passenger terminal is now the Cité de la Mer, a celebration of seafaring heritage, with attractions including nuclear submarine *Le Redoutable*, naval museum and a fabulous aquarium. The town has a life of its own, too, with theatre and restaurants grouped around the place Général de Gaulle, a pleasant pedestrianised shopping centre, and hotels and cafés overlooking the port and fishing boats. An eclectic collection in the **Musée d'Ethnographie**, set in tropical gardens, illustrates cultures and societies from around the world, including the life of the Inuit (Eskimo). Above the town, Fort du Roule, the scene of fierce fighting in 1944, houses a museum about the war years.

In Tourlaville, 5km southeast of Cherbourg, the château (open all year) was the setting for a 16th-century sex scandal, when Julien and Marguerite Ravalet, children of the owners, ran off together and lived as lovers until they were convicted of incest and executed in 1603.

✚ 80B5
🍽 Choice of restaurants along quai de Caligny (€–€€)
🚌 From St-Lô
🚆 Seven per day from Évreux and Caen (on line from Paris St Lazare)
↔ Cap de la Hague (➤ 82)

Cité de la Mer
✉ Gare Maritime Transatlantique
☎ 08 25 33 50 50
🕐 Feb–May, mid-Sep–Dec, 10–6; Jun–mid-Sep, 9:30–7
♿ Good
💶 Expensive

✚	80B3
🍴	Choice of restaurants and cafés (€–€€)
🚌	From Cherbourg
↔	Château de Gratot (▶ 85)

Musée Quesnel-Morinière

✉	2 rue Quesnel-Morinière
☎	02 33 45 11 92
🕐	Daily except Tue and Sun morning. Jul–Aug 10–12, 2–6; Jan–Jun and Sep–Dec 10–12, 2–5 Closed public hols
♿	None
💷	Cheap

Above: *the hilltop spires of Coutances*

COUTANCES ✪✪✪

The Gothic spires of the cathedral soar above the town on its outcrop overlooking the Soulles river. The present church, completed in 1274 with two graceful 80m steeples and a 57m octagonal lantern tower, replaced the Romanesque cathedral built by Bishop Geoffroy de Montbray in the mid-11th century. Inside, the eye is drawn upwards by the tall arcades, past lancet windows and stained glass to the vault, while light pours in through the side-chapel windows. The life of Thomas à Becket and the Day of Judgement are depicted in the magnificent transept windows.

Coutances is a peaceful and prosperous town, with public gardens laid out on the hillside above the Bulsard tributary and the three remaining arches of its 14th-century aqueduct. The 17th-century Hôtel Poupinel at the garden's entrance houses the **Musée Quesnel-Morinière**, with a fine collection of paintings, furniture and dress.

GRANVILLE ⭐⭐

Granville is a town with a many-sided character. There's the busy port with its lively fishing fleet, a terminal for ferries to the Channel Islands, and then there is the boisterous summer resort with shops, restaurants, and the modern Aquarium du Roc that houses a 'shell wonderland' and butterfly garden (▶ 111).

On the narrow headland above the modern town lies the Haute Ville, entered through a grim gateway (Grande Porte) complete with chained drawbridge. The upper town's ramparts were built by the English in the 15th century; within, houses huddle along the grid of streets that leads to the granite Église Notre-Dame and, behind it, are the former barracks. Stone steps just inside the Grande Porte climb up to the **Musée du Vieux Granville** that contains artefacts illustrating the history of the port.

Beyond the walls, the lighthouse on the Pointe du Roc offers good views; northeast, Christian Dior's childhood home has changing exhibits about the designer.

Boats travel to the nearby Îles Chausey, once quarried for granite. Just under 2km long, Grande Île is large enough for a small hotel, a 19th-century fort built against British attack, and a lighthouse.

🔲	80B2
🍴	Choice of restaurants on harbourside (€–€€€)
🚌	From Cherbourg
🚉	Four per day from Argentan (Paris Montparnasse line)
↔	Carolles (▶ 82), Abbaye de Lucerne (▶ 86)

Musée du Vieux Granville

✉	2 rue Lecarpentier
☎	02 33 50 44 10
🕐	Apr–Jun, Wed–Sun 10–12, 2–6; Jul–Sep, Wed–Mon 10–12, 2–6; Oct–Mar, Wed and weekends 2–6
♿	None
💰	Cheap

GRATOT, CHÂTEAU DE ⭐⭐

Hidden behind a church in quiet farmland are the remains of this château built between the 14th and 18th centuries. The site was later used as farm buildings until renovation by volunteers in the 1960s. A roofless main hall, with a fireplace, is flanked by two towers, one of which – the octagonal Tour à la Fée (Fairy Tower) – is decorated with carved foliage and gargoyles, and topped with a delicate stone trellis. Behind the hall, an arched bridge leads across the moat and steps climb to an empty field, once formal gardens. The château was the home of the Argouges family, and an exhibition in the outbuildings tells their story, including an artist's impression of the gardens in their former glory.

🔲	80B3
☎	02 31 57 18 30
🕐	All year daily 10–7
🍴	Le Tourne-Bride (€€), between Gratot and Coutances, on D44
♿	Few
💰	Moderate (pay at coin box in gatehouse)
↔	Coutances (▶ 84)

HAMBYE, ABBAYE DE ⭐

Founded in 1145 by Guillaume Paynel, the Abbaye de Hambye is now a fragile ruin in the tranquil valley of the Sienne. The transept tower survives intact and appears to balance precariously on delicate arches; flying buttresses and the nave's high lancet windows add to the impression that the whole structure could be blown away on the wind. Outbuildings house Rouen tapestries, sculptures, frescos, and paintings of the abbey.

🔲	80C2
☎	02 33 61 76 92
🕐	Guided tours: Apr–Oct, 10–12, 2–6. Closed Tue in winter
🍴	Auberge de l'Abbaye (€€–€€€), on D51 near by
💰	Moderate

+ 80B3

🍴 Limited choice in town (€); or southeast on D900 and south on D57 to le Mesnilbus, Auberge des Bonnes Gens (€–€€€)

🚌 From Cherbourg

↔ Château de Pirou (▶ 87)

Above: the east apse of the abbey church, Lessay

+ 80B2

☎ 02 33 48 83 56

🕐 Daily, mid-Feb–Mar, Oct–Dec, 10–12, 2–5:30; Apr–Sep, 10–12, 2–6:30. Closed Tue in Feb, Mar, Dec

🍴 Auberge le Courtil de la Lucerne (€€)

♿ None

💵 Moderate

↔ Granville (▶ 85)

LESSAY ⊕⊕

Lessay's abbey, Ste-Trinité, was founded in 1056 by Turstin Haldup, lord of la Haye-du-Puits to the north, and completed early in the 12th century. The ancillary monastic buildings suffered in the Hundred Years and Religious wars, and, having been completely rebuilt in the 18th century, were destroyed in 1944. The restored church, however, survives as a fine example of Romanesque architecture, with glowing limestone walls and roof tiles covered in golden lichen. There are three tiers to the nave, with a gallery connecting the uppermost windows. Subdued stained glass adds to the simple tranquillity.

LUCERNE, ABBAYE DE ⊕

Since 1959 the ruins of this 12th-century abbey in the isolated Thar Valley have undergone gradual restoration. The monastic church, used for concerts in the summer, has a Romanesque doorway and an elaborate 18th-century organ. There are also remains of a 19th-century aqueduct, built for a mill in the grounds, along with the tithe barn, abbot's house and dovecote. An arcaded Romanesque lavatorium – a monastic washstand – survives near the old refectory. Sunday mass is still held in the church.

LE MONT-ST-MICHEL (▶ 24–25, TOP TEN)

MORTAIN ✪

Mortain occupies a high ridge overlooking the steep Sélune Valley and Forêt de Mortain. The stark bell tower of Église St-Évroult rises above the main street; inside, the church treasury houses an 8th-century casket, the Chrismale, a reliquary decorated with angels and runic script, probably made in one of the English kingdoms. North of the centre, the buildings of the 12th-century **Abbaye Blanche** are actually dark and stern, despite the name. A walk from the abbey leads to two waterfalls – the Grande and Petite Cascade.

🔒 80C1
🍴 Bars and restaurants in town (€–€€)
↔ Vire (▶ 89)

Abbaye Blanche
☎ 02 33 79 47 47
🕑 Wed–Sun, mid-Jun–Sep, 10–12, 2:30–6. Closed Sun am
♿ Free

The Romanesque cloister arcade at the Abbaye Blanche, Mortain

PIROU, CHÂTEAU DE ✪✪

A gatehouse and castellated walkway lead to substantial ruins in remote farmland near the dunes of the western Cotentin. Ramparts protect the various medieval buildings, stacked up on a moated bailey, including the chapel, bakehouse, kitchens and guardroom; a modern tapestry in the knights' hall relates the Norman conquest of southern Italy and Sicily.

🔒 80B3
☎ 02 33 46 34 71
🕑 Daily Apr–Sep, 10–12, 2–6:30; Feb, Mar, Oct, Nov, 10–12, 2–5. Closed Tue (winter), Dec, Jan
🍴 Bar (€) in Pirou
♿ Moderate

ST-LÔ ✪

Following the bombardment of 1944 that destroyed most of its buildings St-Lô has been rebuilt as a modern town, but with a distinct character of its own. The old town walls survive in part and a single tower guards one corner of the central place Général-de-Gaulle. Market stalls set up under the roof of the tourist office; the office itself allows access to a modern tower giving views over the Vire Valley. The west front of the Église Notre-Dame has been left in its bomb-damaged state, the modern bronze doors a telling contrast to the battered 13th- to 17th-century façade; within, photographs show the extent of the wartime devastation. The Musée des Beaux Arts in the Centre Culturel Jean Lurçat has a collection of paintings and 16th-century tapestries.

🔒 80C3
🍴 Choice of restaurants and bars (€–€€)
🚌 From Cherbourg
🚆 Two per day from Caen

Did you know ?

When the White Ship went down off Barfleur in 1120, it took with it William 'Atheling', son of Henry I of England, signalling the end of the Norman dynasty. Every year, throughout the night of 24–25 November, the bell at Lucerne tolls in mourning.

ST-VAAST-LA-HOUGUE

Cafés overlook the harbour of this cheerful seaside town, famous for its oysters, where yachts and fishing boats jostle for space. Silhouetted at the tip of the southern causeway is Vauban's Fort de la Hougue. At the far end of a wharf is the Chapelle des Marins, a simple stone seamen's chapel with geometric carvings over the doorway. A bird sanctuary and the Musée Maritime of Tatihou Island lie across a narrow channel.

STE-MÈRE-ÉGLISE ⓧ

In a modern building near the market place, the Musée des Troupes Aéroportées commemorates the night of 5 June 1944 when paratroops were dropped over Ste-Mère-Église to support the American army. Among them was Private John Steel, whose parachute became entangled on the church steeple; he hung there for two hours until captured by German soldiers. Each summer a dummy parachutist is suspended from the steeple. A 16th-century farm on the edge of town, the Ferme-Musée du Cotentin, has displays about local rural life.

VALOGNES

The modern centre of Valognes, built after the war, is unremarkable, but the older quarter beyond has real charm. Mellow stone houses back on to a stream crossed by footbridges; one of them, the 15th-century Logis du Grand Quartier, houses the Musée Régional du Cidre et du Calvados, which tells the story of cider-making. Fragments of Roman buildings stand in a pleasant garden, and some grand 17th- to 18th-century houses survive, including the Hôtel de Granval-Caligny, home of 19th-century writer Jules Barbey d'Aurevilly, and the Hôtel de Beaumont, a graceful building with formal gardens.

Polished work by a coppersmith in Villedieu-les-Poëles

VILLEDIEU-LES-POËLES ⬤⬤

Copper pots and tin pans fill the shop windows of Villedieu's long main street (*poêles* means 'pans'). This has been a metalworking centre since the 12th century when the Knights Hospitallers (later 'of Malta') were established in the town. An alley leads from the main street between dark granite houses to the Maison de l'Étain (House of Pewter), while opposite is the Atelier du Cuivre (copper workshop). Bells are still cast in the **Fonderie de Cloches**, set on an island in the Sienne. There are yet more attractions crowded into the little town: a lace-making museum; a clockmaker's workshop; and the Maison du Meuble Normand, across the Sienne behind the main street, with a collection of traditional Norman furniture.

VIRE ⬤

This major route junction in a bend of the Vire river is visited by an endless stream of traffic. At place 6 Juin 1944 cars besiege the 13th-century gate and belfry, the **Porte-Horloge**. There are few other survivors of the historic town that was devastated in World War II: among shops south of the gateway are two defensive towers, and on an eminence above the river are remains of a 12th-century donjon. Local traditions are recalled in the Musée de Vire, set in the quiet cobbled courtyard of the Hôtel-Dieu.

Textile mills once dotted the surrounding *bocage*. Here during the 15th century, in the district known as Vaux de Vire, Olivier Basselin penned his popular poems and songs, the precursors of vaudeville.

Left: a reminder of World War II in the Musée des Troupes Aéroportées, Ste-Mère Église

Sidebar

🔲 80C2
🍴 Restaurants, bars (€–€€)
🚌 From Granville/Argentan/Vire (Paris Montparnasse line)
↔ Abbaye de Hambye (▶ 85)

Fonderie de Cloches
✉ Atelier Cornille Harvard, 10 rue du Pont Chignon
☎ 02 33 61 00 56
🕐 Feb–Jun, Sep–Nov, Tue–Sat, 10–12:30, 2–5:30; Jul, Aug, daily, 9–6
💶 Moderate

🔲 50A3
🍴 Choice of restaurants and cafés (€–€€€)
🚌 From Caen
🚆 Four per day from Granville/Argentan (Paris Montparnasse line)
↔ Mortain (▶ 87)

Porte-Horloge
✉ place du 6 Juin 1944
☎ 02 31 66 28 50 (tourist office)
🕐 Jul to mid-Sep, Mon–Sat 2:30–6:30
💶 Cheap

A Drive Through the Vallée de la Vire

Distance
75km

Time
About 2½ hours without stops

Start point
St-Lô
50A4

End point
Vire
50A3

Lunch
Auberge de la Chapelle (€)
Troisgots, north of la-Chapelle-sur-Vire
02 33 56 32 83

This route winds up and down the green Vire Valley, through peaceful *bocage* countryside.

Take the N174 from St-Lô (➤ 87) to Torigni-sur-Vire.

This fast road sweeps through wooded, rolling farmland to Torigni, a small town with a camping site and lakes, where the Château des Matignon has a display of 17th- and 18th-century tapestries and sculptures.

At the junction by the château, turn right (Tessy-sur-Vire). Cross the roundabout and turn right just before the water tower; then follow signs left, through Brectouville, and right to Roches de Ham.

The road climbs gradually past farms and orchards to this spectacular 80m viewpoint looking down over the curving river and its valley.

Return down the D551 to a right turn (D396), crossing the Vire and climbing the other side of the valley. Turn left to Troisgots and la-Chapelle-sur-Vire.

Pilgrims still come to la Chapelle's riverside church to see its 15th-century statue of Our Lady of Vire; on the opposite bank an ornate gateway and steps lead to the Stations of the Cross.

Turn left with the D159/D359, crossing the river again. At a junction, turn right to Tessy-sur-Vire. Then take the D374/D21 (signed Vire) through Pont-Farcy, and turn left (D307) to Ste-Marie-Outre-l'Eau. The road swings left round the church. Follow the D307 past the Pont-Bellenger turning for the D185 to Campeaux. Join the N174 (right, to Vire), then turn left (D293) and follow the river to the D56 (right) and le Bény-Bocage.

There are good views of the upper Vire Valley from this attractive town, and several viewpoints near by.

After leaving le Bény-Bocage turn right (D577) and continue to Vire (➤ 89).

Where To...

Above: *a colourful display of Camembert cheese labels*
Right: *treats on offer from the local* boulanger

- Tarte d'Yport
- Nid d'Abeilles
- Gâteau Basque
  Beignet Framboise
- Chiquettes
- Crêpes
- Pain Bagnat
- Pain Briard
- Tourte "Maupassant"
- Nouillette
- Pain Brioche

Rouen

Prices

Ratings are based on a three-course meal for one, without wine:

€ = up to €15
€€ = €15–38
€€€ = over €38

Fast Food

The rue des Carmes is a lively Rouen street of shops, hotels and quick-and-cheap eateries. Try the self-service restaurant Funch, at No 60 (☎ 02 35 71 81 81), or Pizza Païfer above it, one of a popular French chain of pizzerias (☎ 02 35 07 73 94).

Al Dente (€)

A respite from the city's fine cuts of meat and creamy cheeses, choose a perfectly cooked pasta dish as a lighter option for both the wallet and the waistline. An unexpected treat in an old half-timbered house.

✉ 24 rue Cauchoise ☎ 02 35 70 24 25 🕔 Lunch, dinner

L'Auberge du Vieux Carré (€€–€€€)

This old-fashioned and intimate restaurant is tucked away off one of the old town's shopping streets. Muted conversation and familiar – though beautifully prepared – dishes. In fine weather the tables are set in a sheltered courtyard; inside, the dining-room is furnished with antiques and paintings.

✉ 34 rue Ganterie ☎ 02 35 71 67 70 🕔 Lunch, dinner. Closed early Aug

Le Beffroy (€–€€)

Straightforward local cooking using cider; good seafood and a choice of game. The setting is a very old building in a quiet street; the atmosphere is smart but animated. A popular choice.

✉ 15 rue Beffroy ☎ 02 35 71 55 27 🕔 Lunch, dinner. Closed Tue and Sun eve

La Boucherie (€€)

Unassuming frontage hides a kitchen skilled in the art of grilling. Steaks prepared to perfection.

✉ 4 place Saint Marc ☎ 02 35 07 70 71 🕔 Lunch, dinner

La Cave Royale (€€)

North African specialities in an atmospheric setting, with colourful pots, scarves and rugs providing decoration around the candlelit tables. For healthy appetites, try the gargantuan Tagine Marakech, a lamb stew with peaches and prunes.

✉ 48 rue Damiette ☎ 02 35 70 63 58 🕔 Lunch, dinner

La Couronne (€€–€€€)

Set in a 14th-century Norman building, this famous restaurant in the historic heart of Rouen claims to be the oldest not only in the city but in France. Gourmets are prepared to pay for the excellent food, but it is possible to sample it at slightly lower prices.

✉ 31 place du Vieux-Marché ☎ 02 35 71 40 90 🕔 Lunch, dinner

Écaille (€€€)

An up-market restaurant near the place du Vieux-Marché, serving delicacies such as lobster salad with ingenious combinations of ingredients. Calvados naturally makes an appearance. One of Rouen's finest seafood restaurants.

✉ 26 rampe Cauchois ☎ 02 35 70 95 52 🕔 Lunch, dinner. Closed Sat and Sun eve, Mon, 8–25 Aug

Les Garamantes (€€)

Traditional Norman dishes of the old days have been supplanted by fashionable Libyan specialities: couscous and Tajines. Eat in or choose takeaway for an exotic picnic.

✉ 4 rue Ste-Croix-des-Pelletiers ☎ 02 35 70 56 83 🕔 Lunch, dinner

Le Grill du Drugstore (€€

A T-bone at the crossroads. Enjoy a traditional meaty lunch at the bustling heart of the city. The wine list complements the menu well.

✉ 2 rue Beauvoisine ☎ 02 35 98 51 20 🕐 Lunch, dinner

Gill (€€–€€€)

Rouennais meals are given a modern touch in this cool, green, modern building by the Seine. Lobster and pigeon are among the offerings; an experience as well as a good meal.

✉ 9 quai de la Bourse ☎ 02 35 71 16 14 🕐 Lunch, dinner. Closed 13–20 Apr, 3–18 Aug, Sun eve in winter, Mon

Gourmand'grain (€–€€)

A pleasant vegetarian option near the cathedral, serving mainly lunches from a counter tucked into the corner of a health-food shop.

✉ 3 rue Petit Salut ☎ 02 35 98 15 74 🕐 Tue–Sat 10–7. Closed Sun, Mon, 25 Dec–1 Jan, 1–20 Aug

Kashemir (€)

Tandoori dishes, classy curries, grills and Naan bread: filling and cheap.

✉ 13 rue Anatole France ☎ 02 35 71 85 89 🕐 Lunch, dinner

Les Maraîchers (€–€€)

Popular old-town restaurant and bistro with tables outside well positioned for watching the world go by. A range of set menus, featuring cheese and meats.

✉ 37 place du Vieux-Marché ☎ 02 35 71 57 73 🕐 Lunch, dinner

Le Maupassant (€–€€)

Hidden amongst the tourist traps on the square by the Joan of Arc church is this lively choice of the younger locals. Dazzling with mirrors and heavily hung with theatrical drapes, what is essentially a bistro is the perfect choice for unwinding after a hard day's shopping.

✉ 39 place du Vieux Marché ☎ 02 35 07 56 90 🕐 Lunch, dinner

Les Nymphéas (€€€)

Upmarket Norman cuisine includes game and fish dishes, plus hot apple and calvados soufflé. Attractive old building with a courtyard, near place du Vieux-Marché.

✉ 7–9 rue de la Pie ☎ 02 35 89 26 69 🕐 Lunch, dinner. Closed 26–30 Aug, Sun eve, Mon

L'Orangerie (€–€€)

An atmospheric, vaulted room and courtyard with plants, statues and a cheerful, comfortable feel. Tables are set outside in spring and summer, and the reasonable menu includes good seafood.

✉ 2 rue Thomas Corneille ☎ 02 35 98 16 03 🕐 Lunch, dinner

Le Panda (€€)

Tucked away off the road with its own courtyard and an entrance guarded by two Chinese lions. A large, efficient restaurant which packs in the customers and serves generous helpings of Chinese and Vietnamese food.

✉ 4 rue Ste-Croix-des-Pelletiers ☎ 02 35 89 82 00 🕐 Lunch, dinner

Restaurant des Beaux-Arts (€€)

Couscous in a variety of forms, plus grilled food and no-nonsense desserts in an old-fashioned but elegant setting complete with uniformed waiters.

✉ 34 rue Damiette ☎ 02 35 70 17 15 🕐 Lunch, dinner

Le Temps des Cerises (€€)

The title may talk of cherries, but the menu shouts of local apples and cheeses. Enjoy the best of Normandy's dairies and orchards at the table and experiment with cheesy *raclettes* and fondues from across France.

✉ 4–6 rue des Basnages ☎ 02 35 89 98 00 🕐 Lunch, dinner

Time for Tea

Salons de thé are found in most sizeable towns – many decked out with chintzy, rather prim furnishings and decor, and some offering an excellent range of herbal and flavoured teas and snacks. Most open mornings and afternoons and serve 'light lunches' which can actually be fairly substantial. The best have a selection of delicious cakes and pastries. For strong, plain tea ask for 'breakfast'; you may need to ask specifically for milk.

The Northeast

Family Feeding

It's not at all unusual to see family groups, including very young children, sitting down to an evening meal in a restaurant. Children are accepted members of the clientele in French eateries, many of which offer quite extensive reduced-price children's menus.

Caudebec-en-Caux
Le Cheval Blanc (€€)

This family run hotel restaurant offers value for money. Truly authentic Normandy cuisine with favourites such as foie gras and Vire Andouille sausages on the menu.

✉ place René Coty ☎ 02 35 96 21 66 🕔 Lunch, dinner. Closed Sun eve

Dieppe
L'Armorique (€–€€)

A first-floor restaurant and ground-floor café attached to a fish shop and overlooking the fishing boats. Generous *assiettes de fruits de mer* come in two quantities, enormous and unbelievable, and the menu ranges from simple and cheap to sophisticated and slightly pricier fish dishes.

✉ 17 quai Henri IV ☎ 02 35 84 28 14 🕔 Lunch, dinner. Closed Sun eve, Mon

Marmite Dieppoise (€–€€)

Located near Église St-Jacques and the harbour, this popular little seafood restaurant serves the local speciality of bowls heaped with a variety of shellfish.

✉ 8 rue St-Jean ☎ 02 35 84 24 26 🕔 Lunch, dinner. Closed mid-Nov to mid-Dec, late Feb to mid-Mar, Thu in winter, Sun eve, Mon

Étretat
L'Huîtrière (€€–€€€)

A conspicuous semicircular building under the Falaise d'Aval, housing a restaurant on two floors. Windows take up the entire wall, allowing panoramic sea views. Seafood is the obvious speciality, and comes in enormous quantities.

✉ rue de Traz Perier ☎ 02 35 27 02 82 🕔 Lunch, dinner

Les Roches Blanches (€€)

A long, low seafood restaurant on the seafront, with wide picture windows, crouching under the cliff at the Falaise d'Amont end of the bay.

✉ terrasse Boudin, front de la mer ☎ 02 35 27 07 34 🕔 Lunch, dinner

Honfleur
Auberge du Vieux Clocher (€€–€€€)

A very smart restaurant in a charming alleyway, with an intimate atmosphere and interesting varieties on the seafood theme, as well as lamb, beef and duck dishes.

✉ 9 rue de l'Homme-de-Bois ☎ 02 31 89 12 06 🕔 Lunch, dinner. Closed Jan, Sun eve, Wed

Le Chat Qui Pêche (€€)

Traditional cuisine from around France's ports at this well-known dining room, blended with good Norman favourites such as duckling and lamb.

✉ 5 place Arthur Boudin ☎ 02 31 89 35 35 🕔 Lunch, dinner

La Cidrerie (€€)

A *crêperie* that prides itself on traditional *galettes* and *crêpes* prepared 'before your very eyes'. Washed down with cider, *poiré*, *pommeau* or calvados, or one of its own creations such as P'tio Punch or l'Épiscopal.

✉ 26 place Hamelin ☎ 02 31 89 59 85 🕔 Lunch, dinner. Closed Wed

Le Corsaire (€–€€)

An intimate dining room in a creamy-yellow old building overlooking the church. Tables are set outside; inside the restaurant is warm and cosy, with an open fire. Squid, chicken in calvados, fish kebabs and guinea fowl braised in calvados among the offerings.

✉ 22 place Ste-Catherine ☎ 02 31 89 12 80 🕐 Lunch, dinner

L'Écluse (€€)

Twin restaurant to Le Chat Qui Pêche (see page 94), popular with visitors to the port and the old town. Reliable fare.

✉ 2 quai de la Quarantaine ☎ 02 31 89 33 33 🕐 Lunch, dinner

Hostellerie Lechat (€€)

An imposing grey-stone building covered in creepers and overlooking the market place and wooden church. Typical Norman dishes and seafood.

✉ 3 place Ste-Catherine ☎ 02 31 14 49 49 🕐 Closed Wed eve and Thu, and Jan to mid-Feb

La Lieutenance (€€)

Outdoor tables in a busy, central position. Good-value lunches and delicious oysters in a straight forward, no-nonsense style.

✉ 12 place Ste-Catherine ☎ 02 31 89 07 52 🕐 Lunch, dinner. Closed Sun eve in winter, also mid-Nov to mid-Dec

Le Pêle-Mêle (€€)

A tea room and *crêperie* that also serves simple meals such as steak and chips, mussels and omelettes. Small and cosy (only six tables); overlooks busy shops through picture windows. Two entrances.

✉ 96 quai Ste-Catherine/4 rue du Dauphin ☎ 02 31 89 50 45 🕐 Closed evenings

Restaurant le Vieux Honfleur (€€–€€€)

An old house full of character beside the harbour, with a timber-framed upper storey, tiled floors and wood panelling. Fresh seafood can be enjoyed on the tables outside.

✉ 13 quai St-Étienne ☎ 02 31 89 15 31 🕐 Lunch, dinner. Closed Jan

Lyons-la-Forêt
Le Grand Cerf (€€)

A restaurant with rooms in an old market-place inn, which serves fresh ingredients with an original touch, including home-baked cakes and puddings.

✉ place de la Halle ☎ 02 32 49 60 44 🕐 Lunch, dinner. Closed Dec–Mar, Tue, Wed

La Licorne (€€–€€€)

A restaurant with rooms in a beautiful old pink-and-brown timber-framed building overlooking the historic market hall. Popular and reliable.

✉ place Bensérade ☎ 02 32 49 62 02 🕐 Lunch, dinner. Closed mid-Dec to mid-Jan, Sun eve, Mon in winter

Le Tréport
Le Homard Bleu (€€)

One of a huge choice of seafood restaurants along the harbour quay, offering cheaper weekday menus.

✉ 45 quai François 1er ☎ 02 35 86 15 89 🕐 Lunch, dinner. Closed Jan to mid-Feb

Villequier
Grand Sapin (€€)

Atmospheric hotel-restaurant with period furniture and balconies overlooking the Seine. Traditional dishes and seafood, using local ingredients. Wood-panelled dining room.

☎ 02 35 56 78 73 🕐 Lunch, dinner. Closed late Nov, mid-Feb to mid-Mar, Tue eve, Wed in winter

Breaking the Habit

The anti-smoking lobby has had some impact even in France, and may well have more effect if anti-smoking legislation is adopted by the French government, but for now you are still unlikely to find an entirely smoke-free area in most restaurants and bars. Be prepared to sit within drifting range as diners whet their appetites or round off a meal with a cigarette or cigar.

Caen & Central Normandy

On the Farm

Traditional home-cooked dishes, served in farmhouses that range from the cosily domestic to the grand historic, are offered in Normandy's *fermes-auberges*. As well as using their own farm produce in their (often very stylish) recipes, some proprietors include tours around the farm. A list of *fermes-auberges* is published by Gîtes de France at Department Tourist Offices (see page 120).

Caen

Alcide (€–€€)

An affordable and popular option in the town centre. Classic French dishes, bistro-style, are served to a loyal local clientele. Generous helpings of mussels, crêpes and meat dishes.

✉ 1 place Courtonne ☎ 02 31 44 18 06 ⏰ Lunch, dinner. Closed late Dec, Sat

La Bourride (€€–€€€)

The most highly regarded restaurant in Caen, with prices to match. Set in one of the older sections of Caen, its decor of copper utensils and flowers complements stone walls and a cosy fire. Regional specialities include Caen *tripes*, chicken in creamy *vallée d'Auge* sauce, Vire chitterlings, pigs' trotters *galette* and other stylish dishes – each guaranteed to have their own added unique touches.

✉ 15–17 rue du Vaugueux ☎ 02 31 93 50 76 ⏰ Lunch, dinner. Closed mid-Aug to 3 Sep, Feb, Sun eve, Mon

Le Cap Horn (€–€€)

The old stone walls and exposed timber beams make this a welcoming choice, especially on a Sunday night out of season. Good range of fish dishes, a reminder of the city's seafaring heritage.

✉ 59 rue Caponière ☎ 02 31 79 37 41 ⏰ Lunch, dinner. Closed Mon

Le Carlotta (€€)

True turn of the century brasserie with a lot of plush soft seating. Blend of traditional dishes, such as steak tartare, with imaginative modern sauces for fresh fish. Huge portions for the larger appetites.

✉ 16 quai Vendeuvre ☎ 02 31 86 68 99 ⏰ Lunch, dinner. Closed Sat, Sun, Aug

Le Crép'uscule (€)

Imaginative, yet unassuming, crêperie. Plenty of salads and an ever changing menu to merit more than one visit even on a short break.

✉ 60 boulevard des Alliés ☎ 02 31 38 84 45 ⏰ Lunch, dinner. Closed Sun dinner, Mon

L'Insolite (€)

Who would have expected a vegetarian menu option in this centuries-old restaurant in the pedestrian quarter, a rare survivor of wartime bombing. Less squeamish diners choose from live lobsters in the dining room.

✉ 16 rue de Vaugueux ☎ 02 31 43 83 87 ⏰ Lunch, dinner. Closed Sun, Mon

La Maison Italie (€)

A small, friendly and informal pizzeria serving the standard fare of Italian and international dishes.

✉ 10 rue Hamon ☎ 02 31 86 38 02 ⏰ Lunch, dinner

La Muscade (€–€€)

Traditional bistro fare and remarkably good prices. Choose from well-cooked clichés, such as *pot au feu* or buckets of mussels. Arrive early if you have not booked as the place is always packed with locals.

✉ 21 place Saint-Martin ☎ 02 31 85 61 84 ⏰ Lunch, dinner

Le Pressoir (€–€€)

A pleasant place with 'olde-worlde' touches and straight-forward dishes, including local favourites such as *boudin noir* and seafood.

✉ 3 avenue Henri-Chéron
☎ 02 31 73 32 71 🕔 Lunch, dinner. Closed Aug, Sun eve, Mon

Le Zodiaque (€€)

Twelve signs of the zodiac in the décor, but even more ways with beef, steaks and duck. Astrological theme apart, a good place for hearty local grills.

☎ 15 quai Eugène-Meslin
🕔 02 31 84 46 31 Lunch, dinner. Closed Sun, hols, Aug

Central Normandy

Alençon

La Couscouserie (€€)

North African cuisine in a small restaurant opposite Église St-Léonard.

✉ 22 rue St-Léonard ☎ 02 33 32 20 26 🕔 Lunch, dinner

Au Petit Vatel (€€)

Locals flock to this friendly restaurant on the edge of town for its charm and good, hearty, traditional food, which includes excellent puddings and an interesting selection of fish dishes.

✉ 72 place Cdt Desmeulles
☎ 02 33 26 23 78 🕔 Lunch, dinner. Closed first three weeks Aug, Sun eve, Wed

La Renaissance (€–€€)

Cool bar for hanging out with Alençon's in-crowd and grabbing a bite before painting the town *rouge*. Open til past midnight, except for Sundays when doors close at 8pm.

✉ 4 rue Saint Blaise ☎ 02 33 26 01 10 🕔 Lunch, dinner

Arromanches-les-Bains

La Marine (€–€€)

A small hotel-restaurant overlooking the port, with good seafood. Customers receive friendly attention, and can expect high standards of cuisine.

✉ 2 quai Canada ☎ 02 31 22 34 19 🕔 Lunch, dinner. Closed mid-Nov to mid-Feb

Balleroy

Manoir de la Drôme (€€€)

Set on the outskirts of the village, this is a top-class restaurant that offers a less pricey set menu. Excellent game and fish dishes and imaginative desserts (try the *tarte au chocolat*) use Norman ingredients but with a stylish flourish.

✉ 129 rue Forges ☎ 02 31 21 60 94 🕔 Lunch, dinner. Closed early Sep, Feb, Sun eve, Mon

Bayeux

Le Lion d'Or (€€–€€€)

An ancient coaching inn near Église St-Jean and assembly rooms. The traditional menu is accompanied by a very good range of wines. A long-established and popular choice with tourists.

✉ 71 rue St-Jean ☎ 02 31 92 06 90 🕔 Lunch, dinner. Closed mid-Dec to mid-Jan, Mon lunch, Sat lunch

Beuvron-en-Auge

Pavé d'Auge (€€–€€€)

Set in a timber-framed market building in the village centre, serving pan-fried oysters, speciality lamb dishes, meat with cider, and calvados soufflé desserts.

✉ place du Village ☎ 02 31 79 26 71 🕔 Lunch, dinner. Closed Dec, early Jul, Tue (Sep–Apr), Mon

Brionne

Auberge du Vieux Donjon (€€)

Excellent restaurant-with-rooms in an 18th-century inn on the main street of the village. Prettily decorated with flowers and warmed by a real fire. The menu includes superb seafood.

✉ 19 rue de la Soie ☎ 02 32 44 80 62 🕔 Lunch, dinner. Closed Mon, Sun eve in winter

Welcome Inn

Another variation on the country cooking theme is the *auberge du terroir*, or country inn. The best of these offer hearty regional cooking, often in buildings which are worth visiting for their own character and setting. Look out for signs (sometimes in the most remote rural areas) directing you to the local inn, or take your pick from the recommended *auberges* within each *département* – details from Gîtes de France (▶ 96, panel).

Brasseries

Less formal and more flexible than traditional restaurants, most brasseries stay open until late at night; some keep going until early morning. Meals are usually quick and filling – and many are excellent, though not necessarily at prices lower than you would expect to pay at a restaurant.

Deauville

L'Augeval (€€–€€€)

Although there are many seafront seafood restaurants in the resort, the best are within the hotels. In summer they serve traditional Norman specialities on the terrace facing the pool.

✉ **15 avenue Hucquart de Turtot** ☎ **02 31 81 13 18** 🕐 **Lunch, dinner**

Dives-sur-Mer

Dupont (€€)

A pretty *pâtisserie* – right next to the church – with a tiny *salon de thé* at the back. Simple meals (pâté, pizza, etc), or take your pick from the delicious offerings in the shop.

✉ **rue Hélène Boucher** ☎ **02 31 91 04 30** 🕐 **Lunch, afternoon tea**

Évreux

Café des Arts (€)

Traditional bar meals, including the obligatory *croque-monsieur/madame* (hefty sandwiches) and a selection of grills and chef's salads. Set in an attractive corner building with views of the belfry and central square.

✉ **5 rue de l'Horloge** ☎ **02 32 31 12 52** 🕐 **Lunch**

Camomille (€€)

A *salon de thé* serving omelettes and generous salads at lunchtimes, plus ice creams and a wide range of speciality teas, in a prettily decorated though slightly cramped room.

✉ **23 rue de Grenoble** ☎ **02 32 38 30 90** 🕐 **Lunch. Closed Sun**

Restaurant Michel Thomas (€–€€)

Norman specialities with an individual touch – duck, veal, and inventive desserts such as spicy fruit puddings. Served in a smart, quiet building on a busy shopping street.

✉ **87 rue Joséphine** ☎ **02 32 33 05 70** 🕐 **Lunch, dinner. Closed Sun**

La Sarrazine (€)

You don't just turn up on the offchance; you need to reserve a table at this very popular crêperie. The food is superb and the cider flows all evening.

✉ **4 rue des Lombards** ☎ **02 32 33 04 60** ✉ **Lunch, dinner. Closed Mon**

Orbec

L'Orbecquoise (€€–€€€)

An intimate restaurant with a log fire, serving stylishly prepared Norman dishes. Reasonable set menus.

✉ **60 rue Grande** ☎ **02 31 62 44 99** 🕐 **Lunch, dinner**

Trouville

La Guinguette (€–€€)

Seafood, fish dishes and *tripes à la mode de Caen* served in a friendly, small restaurant with pavement tables, overlooking the river and fishing boats.

✉ **50–52 quai Fernand Moureaux** ☎ **02 31 88 42 80** 🕐 **Lunch, dinner**

La Marine (€–€€)

Mussels, crabs, prawns and other seafood in a restaurant opposite the fish market. Stone and brick walls; dark, traditional decor.

✉ **146 boulevard Fernand Moureaux** ☎ **02 31 88 12 51** 🕐 **Lunch, dinner**

Les Mouettes (€–€€)

Quiet corner restaurant, away from the river and beach. Good seafood.

✉ **9–11 rue des Bains** ☎ **02 31 98 06 97** 🕐 **Lunch, dinner**

La Moulerie (€–€€)

All manner of *moules*, including *moules Normande*, in a riverside restaurant.

✉ **76 boulevard Fernand Moureaux** ☎ **02 31 81 59 00** 🕐 **Lunch, dinner**

The Northwest

Barfleur

Hôtel Moderne (€€)
Restaurant-with-rooms serving salmon dishes, oysters and goat's cheese *millefeuille*. Cheaper set menu during the week.

✉ 1 place De Gaulle ☎ 02 33 23 12 44 🕐 Lunch, dinner. Closed mid-Jan to mid-Mar, Wed mid-Sep to mid-Jan, Tue Sep–Jun

Barneville-Carteret

Hôtel de la Marine (€€€)
Pricey but stylish hotel-restaurant; oysters with innovative sauces, local lamb, and vanilla butter with cinnamon and sweet cider.

✉ 11 rue de Paris ☎ 02 33 53 83 31 🕐 Lunch, dinner. Closed Sun eve and Mon Feb, Mar and Oct (open Mon lunch in Jul, Aug)

Cherbourg

Café de Paris (€–€€)
Live lobsters in tanks; good range of seafood dishes and a good-value set menu in this café overlooking the port.

✉ 40 quai de Caligny ☎ 02 33 43 12 36 🕐 Lunch, dinner. Closed early Nov

Le Grandgousier (€€–€€€)
Stylish but friendly service. Classy touches to a wide range of seafood options, including caviar, crab claws, shellfish and salmon.

✉ 21 rue de l'Abbaye ☎ 02 33 53 19 43 🕐 Lunch, dinner. Closed Sat lunch, Sun eve

Hôtel La Régence (€€)
Restaurant in the hotel of the same name. Straightforward fish and meat dishes served in brasserie-style room with large windows.

✉ 42 quai de Caligny ☎ 02 33 43 05 16 🕐 Lunch, dinner. Closed 25 Dec–1 Jan

Granville

Citadelle (€€)
Splendid views across the harbour from this popular eatery with a covered terrace. Seafood a speciality, as is the Norman country fare.

✉ 34 rue du Port ☎ 02 33 50 34 10 🕐 Lunch, dinner. Closed Tue (and Wed Oct–Mar)

Horizon (€€)
The restaurant at the Hotel des Bains is as classy as one would expect of a resort dining room, yet menus range from budget value to adventurous seafood treats.

✉ 19 rue Georges Clemenceau ☎ 02 33 50 17 31 🕐 Lunch, dinner

Le Mont-St-Michel

Hôtel la Croix Blanche (€–€€)
A well-placed hotel-restaurant with good food at reasonable prices, and omelettes to compete with the famous Poulard version (see below).

✉ Grande Rue ☎ 02 33 60 14 04 🕐 Lunch, dinner. Closed mid-Nov to Dec

La Mère Poulard (€€–€€€)
Famous hotel-restaurant, with renowned omelettes made to the recipe devised by Mme Poulard in the late 19th century. Bay views.

✉ Grande Rue ☎ 02 33 60 14 01 🕐 Lunch, dinner

St Vaast la Hougue

Les Fuschias (€€)
One of the most popular Logis restaurants in Normandy. Home cooking with a professional flair.

✉ 20 rue Maréchal Foch 🕐 02 33 54 42 26 🕐 Lunch, dinner. Closed Mon (Jul, Aug), Mon, Tue rest of year. Jan, Feb.

Get Set
Restaurants tend to display a range of set menus (*menus fixes*) outside; don't be afraid to study the options before committing yourself. Even the most up-market places may offer quite reasonably priced menus, with a fixed number of courses and a limited choice (the cheaper the menu, the less choice you have). Some include wine and coffee. Weekday lunchtime menus can often give exceptionally good value.

Rouen

Prices

Ratings are based on prices per room, per night.

€	=	under €40
€€	=	€40–90
€€€	=	over €90

Gîtes de France

If you prefer to get off the hotel-motel circuit, it's worth looking at the different types of accommodation offered by Gîtes de France. These include houses or cottages (*gîtes*), often with real character and charm, in isolated rural areas or on the coast, which you can rent for self-catering weeks or a weekend. Details are available from Gîtes de France at the Departmental Tourist Offices (► 120).

Le Bristol (€€)

Overlooking the Palais de Justice and near the rue du Gros-Horloge. Comfortable rooms and parking – a great asset in this largely pedestrianised part of town.

✉ 45 rue aux Juifs ☎ 02 35 71 54 21

Le Dandy (€€)

Well positioned on the rue Cauchoise, leading off to the north of the place du Vieux-Marché, this small hotel is handy for the old-town sights. No restaurant, but near the most popular eateries.

✉ 93 rue Cauchoise ☎ 02 35 07 32 00

Hôtel des Arcades (€–€€)

A good basic hotel in a busy street lined with shops and fast-food restaurants. Some rooms have bath or shower, others just a toilet and bidet.

✉ 52 rue des Carmes ☎ 02 35 70 10 30

Hôtel de la Cathédrale (€€)

An old building with a pretty courtyard and green-and-white decor, near the cathedral and archbishop's palace. Not easily accessible by car, but a place of genuine character – among some of Rouen's best medieval houses – and run with friendly, attentive charm. No restaurant.

✉ 12 rue St-Romain ☎ 02 35 71 57 95

Hôtel de Dieppe (€€€)

As you would expect from a Best Western hotel, you get all the mod cons, but there's also a highly reputable restaurant, Le Quatre Saisons.

✉ place B Tissot ☎ 02 35 71 96 00

Hotel du Havre (€)

Just eight rooms in this homely hotel above a traditional old-fashioned bar with its zinc counter and basic meals. Convenient for the station.

✉ 27 rue Verte ☎ 02 35 71 46 43

Hôtel Mercure Rouen Centre (€€€)

A discreetly up-market hotel in the Mercure chain, with a large, open lobby behind sliding doors in a narrow old-town street. Facilities include a private garage and all mod cons in the rooms. No restaurant.

✉ 7 rue Croix-de-Fer ☎ 02 35 52 69 52

Hôtel de Québec (€–€€)

Good value in this comfortable hotel run with efficiency; particularly popular with British visitors.

✉ 18–24 rue du Québec ☎ 02 35 70 09 38 🕐 Closed 23 Dec–3 Jan

Hôtel le Viking (€€)

A good bet for an overnight stay. Set on a busy riverside road, but rooms at the rear, overlooking the bus station, are much quieter. Small clean and convenient rooms with all the basics; helpful service. Locked underground garage.

✉ 21 quai du Havre ☎ 02 35 70 34 95

La Tour de Beurre (€)

Basic budget accommodation with the heady scent of crepes and gallettes wafting through open windows from the street counter below.

✉ 20 quai Pierre Corneille ☎ 02 35 71 95 17

The Northeast

Les Andelys

Hôtel de Paris (€€)
A handsome, red-brick 19th-century building on the approach road into Grand Andely, with a restaurant.

✉ 10 avenue de la République ☎ 02 32 54 00 33 ⑤ Closed Feb

Caudebec-en-Caux

Le Cheval Blanc (€€)
Charming Logis de France hotel by the Seine on the Abbeys' circuit. Friendly welcome and pleasant restaurant.

✉ Place René Coty ☎ 02 35 96 21 66 ⑤ Closed late Dec

Hôtel de Normandie (€–€€)
An established hotel-restaurant (Logis de France) with rooms overlooking the river; reasonably priced.

✉ 19 quai Guilbaud ☎ 02 35 96 25 11

Normotel-La Marine (€€)
Balconied hotel-restaurant with good views of the Seine. Parking.

✉ 18 quai Guilbaud ☎ 02 35 96 20 11

Clères

Le Tôt (€€)
Bed and breakfast in one double room, in Véronique Degonse's turn-of-the-century home surrounded by 3ha of wooded grounds. Cycle hire.

✉ 76690 Clères ☎ 02 35 33 34 38

Duclair

Hôtel de la Poste (€€–€€€)
A Logis de France on the Seine quayside. Good first-floor restaurant and a friendly atmosphere.

✉ 286 quai de la Libération ☎ 02 35 05 92 50

Étretat

Domaine St Clair (€€–€€€)
Swim year round in the heated outdoor pool, where you can gaze up at the ivy covered turrets of this impressive hotel. Splash out on a four-poster bed and magnificent views or settle for something more modest, but still comfortable, in what is, after all, a true château-hotel. Ideal for special occasions or pampering indulgence. Facilities for disabled guests.

✉ Chemin de St Clair ☎ 02 35 27 08 23

Hôtel Dormy House (€€–€€€)
You get great sea views from this Logis de France, which has its own restaurant.

✉ Route du Havre ☎ 02 35 27 07 88

L'Escale (€€)
A no-frills hotel, which represents great value. Attractive rooms and a small restaurant serving simple meals. Sea views.

✉ Place Foch ☎ 02 35 27 03 69

Hôtel les Falaises (€–€€)
No sea view, but comfortable, clean rooms in a central position, by the *halles*. The pink neon sign is unmissable.

✉ 1 boulevard René Coty ☎ 02 35 27 02 77

Hôtel de la Poste (€€)
Simple but efficient hotel offering good value on the town's main road. There is a garden.

✉ 6 avenue George V ☎ 02 35 27 01 34

Bed and Breakfast

Bed and breakfast is offered in a growing number of private homes, farms, manor houses and even châteaux. Known as *chambres d'hôtes*, they are graded by Gîtes de France in *épis*, or ears of corn: one for simple rooms with basin and shared bathroom; two for comfier rooms with bath or shower and shared toilet; three for fully en-suite rooms; and four for especially comfortable, well-equipped rooms of particular character. Brochures are available from Gîtes de France (▶ 100, panel).

101

For the Children

Another variation on the *gîtes* theme is the Gîtes d'Enfants. Members of this scheme welcome children aged between six and twelve into their own families, offering them the opportunity of sampling life in the French countryside. Details from Gîtes de France (➤ 100).

Eu
La Cour Carrée (€€)
Bright clean bedrooms and spacious bathrooms in a value for money hotel. Big breakfast buffet to start the day.
✉ Route de Dieppe ☎ 02 35 50 60 60

Domaine de Joinville (€€€)
One for special occasions, a *château-hôtel* with tennis, pool, gardens and a gym. Rooms are expensive but the restaurant has reasonably priced options. Meals can be eaten outside on the terrace.
✉ route du Tréport, 1km west ☎ 02 35 50 52 52

Hotel Maine (€–€€)
Comfortable rooms in a revived Logis de France near the railway station. Parking available.
✉ 20 place de la Gare ☎ 02 35 86 16 64 🕔 Closed 15 Aug–8 Sep

Gisors
Hostellerie des Trois Poissons (€€)
Impressive timber-framed building on the lively main street, between the church and the château.
✉ 13 rue Cappeville ☎ 02 32 55 01 09 🕔 Summer (except last half of Jun) until Oct.

Le Havre
Clarine Hôtel-Restaurant (€€)
A sprawling glass building near the main road and harbour, with a McDonald's next door. Rooms offer good facilities and convenience for travellers.
✉ quai Colbert ☎ 02 35 26 49 49

Honfleur
L'Absinthe (€€€)
An up-market and expensive hotel set in a former 16th-century presbytery in the old town. Comfortable, characterful rooms with exposed beams. The restaurant has reasonably priced set menus.
✉ 10 quai de la Quarantaine ☎ 02 31 89 23 23 🕔 Closed 14 Nov–31 Dec

Hôtel Campanile (€€)
Modern motel-style accommodation with restaurant, on the D579 just outside town. Buffet breakfasts, en-suite bedrooms with coffee- and tea-making facilities, rooms for visitors with disabilities, and non-smoking rooms. Plenty of free parking.
✉ le Poundreux Route de Paris ☎ 02 31 89 13 13

Hôtel des Cascades (€€)
Set back from the Vieux Bassin on a cobbled street, this hotel offers reasonably priced rooms. There is a good-value restaurant.
✉ 17 place Thiers (cours de Fossés) ☎ 02 31 89 05 83 🕔 Closed 12 Nov–14 Feb

Hotel Cheval Blanc (€€–€€€)
Rather special hotel in a historic 15th-century building overlooking the fishing port. Comfortable rooms and babysitting service available.
✉ 2 quai des Passagers ☎ 02 31 81 65 00 🕔 Closed Jan

Otelinn (€€)
A modern hotel with comfortable, small rooms and a traditional-style restaurant serving local dishes. About a kilometre from the Vieux Bassin. Free parking.
✉ 62 cours Albert-Manuel ☎ 02 31 89 41 77

Le Tréport
Le Saint-Yves (€–€€)
A friendly, traditional resort hotel with flowery decor and a restaurant serving good-value seafood.
✉ 7 place Albert Cauët ☎ 02 35 86 34 66 🕔 Closed mid-Dec to mid-Jan

Caen & Central Normandy

Caen

Au Saint-Jean (€–€€)
Good-value rooms with no frills but all basic facilities; helpful staff and its own garage. Near the Église St-Jean, south of the château.
✉ **20 rue des Martyrs**
☎ **02 31 86 23 35**

Central Hôtel (€)
A hotel that lives up to its name, being well placed in the city centre, with views of the château from some rooms. Cheap and basic, but convenient. No restaurant.
✉ **23 place J Letellier** ☎ **02 31 86 18 52**

Hôtel des Cordeliers (€–€€)
Wide range of rooms with a choice of prices – choose what best suits your budget. Set in its own garden.
✉ **4 rue des Cordeliers** ☎ **02 31 86 37 15**

Hôtel le Dauphin (€€–€€€)
A restored 18th-century priory with rooms in the old building and a modern annexe. Traditional, country-style restaurant and separate breakfast room. Handy for the town centre. Car park.
✉ **29 rue Gémare** ☎ **02 31 86 22 26**

Hôtel du Havre (€–€€)
Budget accommodation with en-suite facilities in a hotel midway between the station and the castle.
✉ **11 rue du Havre** ☎ **02 31 86 19 80**

Mercure Caen Centre (€€€€)
High prices for reliable en-suite rooms with all the trappings, including colour TV with international channels, minibars. Buffet breakfasts, atrium bar. On a square at the northern end of the Pleasure Port.
✉ **1 place Courtonne**
☎ **02 31 47 24 24**

Hôtel Moderne (€€–€€€)
Set in the long boulevard leading into the place St-Pierre (for the tourist office and church), this pleasant hotel also has its own car park. Not particularly modern in appearance, though, and difficult to reach by car: ask for directions. No restaurant.
✉ **116 boulevard Maréchal Leclerc** ☎ **02 31 86 04 23**

Hôtel Otelinn (€€)
Close to the Mémorial museum, 25km outside Caen, this hotel has a reliable restaurant and is a good overnight choice for those making a day of the tour and keen for an early start out of town.
✉ **Avenue Montgomery**
☎ **02 31 44 34 00**

Hôtel Saint-Étienne (€)
A good budget choice with character, set in an 18th-century stone building within reach of the Abbaye aux Hommes. Some rooms without showers.
✉ **2 rue de l'Académie** ☎ **02 31 86 35 82**

Hôtel de l'Univers (€–€€)
Small and basic motel near the quayside, with rather drearily decorated but clean rooms, some sharing toilet facilities. Set on a large and busy square with plenty of public parking.
✉ **12 quai Vendeuvre, place Courtonne** ☎ **02 31 85 46 14**

Laying on the Charm
If money is no object, consider spending on a stay in Normandy's up-market 'hotels of charm' set in grand châteaux, rambling country inns, converted mills or turreted manor-houses. Many have gourmet restaurants, too. A booklet called *Hôtels-Restaurants de Charme en Normandie* is published by the Comité Régional de Tourisme de Normandie at Le Doyenné, 14 rue Charles Corbeau, Évreux (☎ 02 32 33 79 00).

Logis de France

Hotels that tag Logis de France or LF after their names are part of a voluntary association – now with over 3,800 members – that guarantees a high level of comfort and service, excellent food, and a pleasant environment. Each hotel's range of facilities is graded with one, two or three *cheminées* (fireplaces). Details are available from the Fédération Nationale des Logis de France, 83 avenue d'Italie, 75013 Paris (☎ 01 45 84 70 00).

Central Normandy

Alençon
Hôtel Le Chapeau Rouge (€–€€)
Convenient and pretty hotel in the heart of town. Some rooms overlooking the adjacent road can be noisy. No restaurant.
✉ 1 and 3 boulevard Duchamp
☎ 02 33 26 20 23 🅘 Closed 1–15 Aug

Hôtel Le Grand St-Michel (€–€€)
Good-value, traditional service in a quiet Logis de France hotel. Restaurant serves generous portions for very reasonable prices.
✉ 7 rue du Temple ☎ 02 33 26 04 77 🅘 Closed Jul

Bayeux
Churchill Hotel (€€–€€€)
In the heart of town, a quiet and welcoming retreat with free parking and individually styled rooms.
✉ 14 rue St-Jean ☎ 02 31 21 31 80 🅘 Closed Jan

Hôtel du Lion d'Or (€€–€€€)
Long-established hotel in an old coaching inn with a courtyard, near the centre. Bright, comfortable rooms and a restaurant.
✉ 71 rue St-Jean ☎ 02 31 92 06 90 🅘 Closed mid-Dec–end Jan

Hôtel Mogador (€€)
A very pleasant hotel tucked in among the shops, with a friendly welcome and good-value rooms, some of which have cooking facilities.
✉ 20 rue Alain Chartier
☎ 02 31 92 24 58

Cabourg
Grand Hôtel (€€€)
An up-market seafront hotel in the grand old tradition, which makes the most of its connections with Proust, and serves *madeleines* (the cakes associated with his *Remembrance of Things Past)* for breakfast.
✉ Promenade Marcel Proust
☎ 02 31 91 01 79

Hôtel de Paris (€–€€)
Central hotel in a timber-framed building, with a wide range of room prices. Parking.
✉ 39 avenue de la Mer
☎ 02 31 91 31 34

Évreux
France (€–€€)
A traditional hotel set in a quiet location within the centre of Évreux. The pleasant rooms are augmented by a very good restaurant offering classic dishes and fine wines.
✉ 29 rue St-Thomas ☎ 02 32 39 09 25

Sées
Hôtel du Cheval Blanc (€–€€)
Some of the rooms at the back of this timber-framed building are rather dark and oppressive. Others are brighter with good views of the cathedral.
✉ 1 place St-Pierre ☎ 02 33 27 80 48 🅘 Closed 16–27 Feb, 11 Nov–31 Dec

Hôtel Le Dauphin (€€)
Logis de France hotel near the old market hall, with good breakfasts and generous evening meals.
✉ 31 place des Halles ☎ 02 33 27 80 07 🅘 Closed Jan

Trouville
Hôtel Carmen (€€)
A small hotel near the beach, with a friendly atmosphere.
✉ 24 rue Carnot ☎ 02 31 88 35 43 🅘 Closed Jan

Hôtel les Sablettes (€€)
Quiet hotel with a garden, near the town centre.
✉ 15 rue P Besson ☎ 02 31 88 10 66

The Northwest

Barneville-Carteret

Hôtel de la Marine (€€€)
Cheerful hotel overlooking the sea and port. Expensive rooms; terrace with parasol tables in summer. Parking and an excellent restaurant.
✉ 11 rue de Paris ☎ 02 33 53 83 31 🕐 Closed 3 Nov–19 Feb

Cherbourg

Ambassadeur Hôtel (€–€€)
Bright, well-designed rooms, double-glazed against the busy port near by. Parking behind the hotel. Restaurant.
✉ 22 quai de Caligny ☎ 02 33 43 10 00 🕐 Closed late Dec

Hôtel Mercure (€€€)
Modern building, strangely isolated beside the port. Convenient for the car ferry, but less so for the town centre and restaurants.
✉ Allée Président Menut ☎ 02 33 44 01 11

Hôtel la Régence (€€–€€€)
Pleasant Logis de France hotel in a white quayside building, with simply furnished rooms, parking at the rear, and a brasserie-style restaurant.
✉ 42 quai de Caligny ☎ 02 33 43 05 16 🕐 Closed 24 Dec–2 Jan

Coutances

Hôtel le Normandie (€–€€)
Small hotel behind the cathedral, with a restaurant (closed Mon in winter, Sun eve) serving good-value meals. Parking.
✉ 2 place Général-de-Gaulle ☎ 02 33 45 01 40

Granville

Hôtel le Grand Large (€€–€€€)
Modern building set on the cliff overlooking the sea; includes a sea-therapy centre. Parking, swimming pool, jacuzzi, restaurant. Wide price range for rooms.
✉ 5 rue de la Falaise ☎ 02 33 91 19 19

Le Mont-St-Michel

Hôtel la Croix Blanche (€€–€€€)
Well-known hotel on the ramparts with spectacular views of the bay, and a restaurant with good-value menus (► 99). Rooms, however, can be expensive.
✉ Intra-Muros ☎ 02 33 60 14 04 🕐 Closed 16 Nov–14 Feb

Hôtel du Mouton Blanc (€€–€€€)
Attractive stone and timber building, with a good restaurant and sea views. The cheapest rooms – by the standards of le Mont-St-Michel – are very reasonable.
✉ Intra-Muros ☎ 02 33 60 14 08

Orbec

Chambres Mme Vaillère (€–€€)
Excellent bed and breakfast in an old house on the main street. Double rooms in an annexe (two share bathroom and toilet) entered through a pretty courtyard. Breakfast served inside or out. Evening meals by arrangement.
✉ 62 rue Grande ☎ 02 31 32 77 99

Villedieu-les-Poëles

Hôtel le Fruitier (€€)
Well-run Logis de France hotel and restaurant, open all year. Modern, comfortable rooms with stylish decor and welcoming staff.
✉ place des Costils ☎ 02 33 90 51 00 🕐 Closed mid-Dec–early Jan

Access to Accommodation

Few tourist sites in Normandy are fully prepared for visitors with disabilities, but there are some associations offering guidance about finding suitable accommodation. *Les Gîtes accessibles aux personnes handicapées* is published by Gîtes de France and is available from 35 rue Godot de Mauroy, 75439 Paris. The *Guide Rousseau*, which covers hotels, bed and breakfast, *gîtes*, and camping sites by *département*, is available from Association France H, 9 rue Luce de Lancival, 77340 Pontault-Combault.

Gifts

Shopping Glossary

la boulangerie bakery, selling the traditional 'stick' bread (*baguette*) plus a wide variety of types of loaf (*pain*)
le boucherie butcher
les cadeaux gifts
la charcuterie ham, sausages, pork and snacks (meat or fish pies)
la chocolaterie/confiserie chocolates and sweetmeats
l'épicerie grocery
la fromagerie cheese shop
la librairie bookshop, newsagent
la pâtisserie pastries, almost always fresh and delicious, ranging from the relatively plain, such as croissants, to the elaborate and creamy
la pharmacie chemist
la poissonerie fishmonger
le tabac tobacconist (also sells stamps)

Rouen

Antiquité Boisnard
This antique shop is almost 100 years old and is an old favourite for choosing that special present.
✉ **54 rue République**
☎ **02 35 70 60 08**

Le Rouennier
Ceramics, vases, knick-knacks and trinkets; all can be gift-wrapped on site.
✉ **56 rue République** ☎ **02 35 70 54 17**

Carpentier Faïencier
The famous blue and white *faïences de Rouen*, once de rigeur at the French court, make excellent presents and stylish souvenirs. This shop and workshop has several unique pieces made on site.
✉ **26 rue St-Romain** ☎ **02 35 88 77 47**

Artisanat
Opposite Église St-Maclou, an upmarket shop specialising in clocks – ceramic, wooden, big and small – and faience gifts.
✉ **Place Barthélemy** ☎ **02 35 71 58 34**

La Fontaine Marmitaine
A very attractive toyshop in a timber-framed building, with displays of rocking horses, puppets, dolls, toy soldiers and teddy bears in its large picture window.
✉ **rue du Gros-Horloge** ☎ **02 35 88 19 99**

Ma Normandie
In the heart of the old town, specialising in faïence (decorated ceramics) in the form of ornaments, pots and plates. Other gifts include pictures and barometers.

✉ **Corner of rue St-Nicolas**
☎ **02 35 71 46 08**

The Northeast

Dieppe
Antiquités Sutton
Antique cutlery, porcelain figures and ivory pieces in a corner shop.
✉ **rue St-Rémy**

Le Comptoir des Isles/Le Gallion
Jewellery and gifts with a maritime theme – toy boats, floating-ship paperweights, and ship wheels and lamps.
✉ **Place Nationale** ☎ **02 35 40 14 18**

La Galerie Montador
Art gallery and children's gift and toy shop, with wooden trains, puppets and bricks, Tintin tee shirts, and grown-ups' gifts such as lamps and ship-shape condiments.
✉ **4 rue Bains** ☎ **02 35 82 63 03**

Spirit of Boudha
Recapture the exoticism of Dieppe's mercantile past with a gift from the Far East.
✉ **77 Grande Rue** ☎ **02 35 40 35 02**

Etretat
Les Perles de Charlotte
Charlotte Le Goff makes more than strings of pearls. Her original jewellery, from bracelets to brooches, is sold in the workshop boutique.
✉ **9 rue Alphonse Karr**
☎ **06 17 71 53 70**

Bazar et Cie
Smart ideas for home decor and stylish gifts.
✉ **12 rue Prosper Brindejont**
☎ **02 35 29 04 03**

Honfleur

Agate
Imaginative, and sometimes bizarre, jewellery.

✉ **21 rue des Logettes**
☎ **02 31 89 53 88**

Le Sémaphore
Ship compasses and bells, lanterns, sailor's caps, porthole mirrors, and other gifts for the seadog who has everything.

✉ **rue des Lingots** ☎ **02 31 89 97 85**

Oriot
Pick up an art deco lamp or a Napoleon III chair. Antiques and collectables from the 18th century to the 1940s in this surprisingly light and airy bright blue corner shop.

✉ **19 rue des Lingots**
☎ **02 31 89 70 04**

Caen

Artagor
Arts and crafts, including mosaic mirrors, painted lamps, hats and jewellery – unusual souvenirs.

✉ **rue Buquet** ☎ **02 31 93 16 00**

Bijoux Pawlak
Antique jewellery is the speciality of this old shop, which also sells superb silver tableware.

✉ **124 rue Basse** ☎ **02 31 93 62 04**

Le Bois Dormant
Wonderful wooden toys and games for children – tops, trains, drums, jigsaws – in the traditional style. Opposite Église St-Sauveur.

✉ **rue Froide** ☎ **02 31 85 35 01**

Family Broc
Open every day of the week, this antique shop is the ideal place for art lovers to pick up a quality memento of a region that has inspired generations of painters.

✉ **223 rue de Bayeux** ☎ **02 31 73 00 01**

Central Normandy

Bayeux

Naphtaline
Inspired by the Bayeux tapestry, buy needlework themed gifts from cushions to kits, napkins to curtains.

✉ **16 parvis de la Cathédrale**
☎ **02 31 21 50 03** 🕐 **Closed Jan Feb and Sun (out of season)**

Weldom Tronsson-Grenier
This is the place for heavy duty le Creuset cookware and other pots, pans and kitchen goodies.

✉ **34 rue Saint Martin** ☎ **02 31 92 09 55** 🕐 **Closed Mon am and Sun**

Évreux

Tentations
Painted wooden ornaments, jewellery, umbrellas and other gift ideas.

✉ **rue Docteur Oursel** ☎ **02 32 31 66 65**

Trouville

Art et Decoration
Painted pots, lights, pictures and gifts, some tacky, others interesting, in a little riverside shop.

✉ **boulevard Fernand-Moureaux**

La Palette
Hematite and crystals, all ready to wear. Jewellery made from minerals and rocks.

✉ **8 rue de Paris** ☎ **02 31 88 13 75**

The Northwest

Cherbourg

A Cosnefroy
Textiles, umbrellas, lamps, dolls; all kinds of everything in a cluttered but welcoming little shop.

✉ **18 rue au Blé** ☎ **02 33 93 19 27**

Markets
Weekly markets take place in many Normandy towns and add considerably to their character and atmosphere.

Alençon (Tue, Thu, Sat, Sun)
Les Andelys (Sat)
Argentan (Tue, Fri, Sun)
Avranches (Sat)
Bayeux (Sat)
Bernay (Sat)
Brionne (Sun)
Caen (Fri, Sun)
Cherbourg (Tue)
Coutances (Thu)
Dieppe (Sat)
Dives-sur-Mer (Tue)
Étretat (Thu)
Eu (Fri)
Évreux (Wed, Sat)
Fécamp (Sat)
Gisors (Mon)
Granville (Sat)
Honfleur (Sat)
Louviers (Sat)
Lyons-la-Forêt (Thu)
Mortain (Sat)
Pont-Audemer (Mon)
St-Lô (Sat)
Ste-Mère-Eglise (Thu)
Sées (Sat)
Trouville (Wed, Sun)
Valognes (Fri)
Verneuil-sur-Avre (Sat)
Villedieu-les-Poëles (Tue)
Vire (Fri)

Fashion

What's in Store
Printemps and Monoprix are department-store chains with outlets all over France. Printemps sells mid-budget clothes, jewellery, shoes and cosmetics; Monoprix sells lower-budget clothes, household goods, cosmetics and food. Stores can be found in Rouen, Évreux, Vernon, Lisieux, Trouville, Caen, Cherbourg and other centres.

Rouen

Catimini
Pretty children's clothes in eye-catching colours and designs; also shoes and accessories.
✉ **50 rue des Carmes** ☎ **02 35 07 18 00**

Eléonore
Stylish girls' outfits in the classiest shopping street in town, handy for most hotels.
✉ **136 rue du Gros-Horloge** ☎ **02 35 07 09 11**

Florence Kooijman
A shoe designer who also has outlets in Lille, le Touquet and Amiens. Elegant shoes and ankle boots in suede or leather at reasonable prices.
✉ **11 rue Ganterie** ☎ **02 35 89 35 81**

Gary Bis
Smart contemporary menswear, at a price. A hint of Parisian style.
✉ **6–8 rue Eugène Boudin** ☎ **02 35 71 96 53**

The Northeast

Honfleur
Anne Fontaine
The designer who all but reinvented the white shirt in *chic couture* is famous for the purity and simplicity of her women's fashions. A cut above the standard *matelot* jerseys in rival windows.
✉ **7 quai Saint-Étienne** ☎ **02 31 89 00 53**

Caline & Coquine
Lingerie and *sous-vetements* with that essential *je ne sais quoi*.
✉ **8 rue de la République** ☎ **02 31 89 02 26**

Caen

Maison du Pantalon
Trousers and jeans for men and women, plus shirts, gloves, ties and accessories.
✉ **35 rue St-Pierre** ☎ **02 31 86 09 17**

Central Normandy

Alençon
Boutique Virginie
Examples of different types of lace, including *point d'Alençon*, and a wide selection of other fabrics.
✉ **146 Grande Rue** ☎ **02 33 26 53 71**

Bayeux
Port Marine
When in Normandy, dress like a local. Buy the caps and stripy tops in this welcoming and friendly seafarers' outfitters.
✉ **22 quai Félix Faure** ☎ **02 31 21 72 83** 🕐 **Closed Wed (except Jul, Aug)**

Trouville
Troc-Chic
Vintage clothes dating from the 1940s to the 1960s.
✉ **80 rue des Bains** ☎ **02 31 81 09 19**

The Northwest

Cherbourg
Gulliver
Smart leather shoes for men and children, including multicoloured suede shoes.
✉ **rue des Fosses** ☎ **02 33 53 83 83**

Studio Mod
Costume jewellery for stylish women.
✉ **rue au Blé** ☎ **02 33 94 06 04**

Food

Rouen

Chocolaterie Auzou

This master chocolate maker in the bustling centre of the city is an essential detour on any walking tour. Delicious hand-made creations to make your mouth water.

✉ 163 rue du Gros-Horloge
☎ 02 35 70 59 31

Héloin Anne-Marie

Delicious sweets, chocolates and other goodies such as *pains d'épices* (gingerbread), jams, marmalades and honey, all beautifully presented.

✉ 98 rue des Carmes ☎ 02 35 71 02 94

The Northeast

Honfleur
La Petite Chine

Fresh pastries, *pains d'épices*, calvados and chocolates; a small tearoom at the back.

✉ Corner of rue du Dauphin and rue de la Foulerie ☎ 02 31 89 36 52

Les Trois Étoiles de Honfleur

This is something special. Choose your liqueur, spirit, oil or vinegar, and then select a bottle for your purchase from an eclectic range of flasks and glass vessels. Unique and memorable gifts for the foodie in your life.

✉ 5 rue Haute ☎ 02 31 89 03 35

Caen

Charlotte Corday

Calvados and apple-flavoured chocolates give the treats at this upmarket sweetshop a very Norman twist.

✉ 114 rue Saint-Jean ☎ 02 31 86 33 25 🕐 Closed Sun, Mon

Aux Fromages de France

The place for scores of cheeses, farmhouse meat dishes and ciders.

✉ 116 rue Saint-Jean
☎ 02 31 86 14 53

Central Normandy

Évreux
La Valeine

Home made ice-cream, cider and goats' cheese from this farm shop on the edge of town.

✉ Manoir de Cateuil, route du Havre ☎ 02 35 27 14 02

Vimoutiers
Musée du Camembert

A statue of Marie Harel, the discoverer of Camembert cheese, contemplates the town square in the cider-producing region of the Pays d'Auge. Vimoutiers was largely rebuilt after World War II and its chief interest for visitors is the museum, dedicated to the much-copied but rarely bettered local soft cheese. The cheese is recognisable for its creamy interior and white crust – perfect with bread and cider.

✉ 10 avenue du Général de Gaulle ☎ 02 33 39 30 29

The Northwest

St-Vaast-la-Hougue
Maison Gosselin

In an unassuming street is one of the finest grocer's shops in the region. From the delicatessen counters serving cheeses and meats to the excellent wine cellars and an enviable range of calvados and whiskies, this family business is marked by a love of fine food and drink.

✉ Rue de Verrüe ☎ 02 33 54 40 06

Fresh from the Farm

It's worth looking beyond the high street for many of the traditional Norman goods. Factories and farm shops are often the best places to sample and buy cheese, cider, honey, calvados, vegetables, fruit, and even durable products such as pottery and wool. For details contact the Comité Régional de Tourisme de Normandie (► 103).

Children's Attractions

Four-legged Friends

Horse-mad children will be in their element in Normandy, one of the foremost breeding centres in the country. The dappled Percheron horses, once bred to pull drays and buses, are still a famous feature of the Perche region; legend has it that their forebears were cobs and Arabs during the time of the crusades. At le Pin-au-Haras (➤ 70), a parade of beautiful horses pulling four-in-hand carriages jingles and trots through the grounds every Thursday at 3 (summer only). A demonstration of American cowboy riding techniques is the star turn at Quarter Horse Dream, at le Vitou, Vimoutiers, open daily (☎ 02 33 39 12 05).

Leisure and Amusement Parks

The Northeast

Bolleville
Trace Viking
Relive the age of the Vikings as you watch traditional settlements being constructed.
✉ Aire de Bolleville on the A29 motorway access road on the N15 ☎ 02 35 21 21 83 🕐 Open May–Sep 10–6 💲 moderate

Clères
Parc du Bocasse
A family park with 80 games and rides, an enchanted river, pedalos, and its very own 'Niagara Falls'.
✉ Southwest of Clères, on D6 ☎ 02 35 33 22 25 🕐 Mid-Mar to Easter, Sep to mid-Oct, Wed and Sat 12–6, Sun and public hols 10–7; Easter hol–early Sep, daily 10–6 💲 Expensive

Gisors
Parc de Loisirs du Bois d'Hérouval
A hundred or so games and activities especially designed for children, just beyond the Normandy border.
✉ 1km south of Gisors, off D915 ☎ 02 32 55 33 76 🕐 May–early Sep 10:30–6 💲 Moderate

Le Havre
Le Canyon
Fifty rides and games include Wild West fun and water slides.
✉ Epretot, 15km northeast of Le Havre, off N15 ☎ 02 35 20 42 69 🕐 Jun–Aug, daily 10:30–7; Mar–May, Sep to mid-Nov, Wed and weekend 💲 Moderate

Caen

Festyland
Plenty of choice for the energetic: bouncy castles, water rides and slides, go-karts, and toboggans.
✉ Bretteville-sur-Odon, outskirts of Caen ☎ 02 31 75 04 04 🕐 First Sun in Apr–last Sun in Sep, daily 11–7 💲 Expensive

The Northwest

Mortain
Parc de Loisirs L'Ange Michel
Laid out over 10ha near the Lac de Vezins. Giant (50m) toboggan, pony rides, children's electric cars and a mini-train.
✉ St-Martin-de-Landelles, south of St-Hilaire-du-Harcouët, on D977 west of Mortain ☎ 02 33 49 04 74 🕐 Jun–Aug, daily from 11; Apr, May, Sep, weekend and public hols from 1:30 💲 Moderate

Model and Tourist Trains

Central Normandy

Clécy
Musée du Chemin de Fer Miniature
Claimed to be one of the largest model railways in Europe. Little locomotives – 220 of them – thunder along 430m of track around a scaled-down version of the Suisse Normande. A slightly larger train carries children round the grounds.
✉ D562, 38km southwest of Caen ☎ 02 31 69 07 13 🕐 Easter–end Sep, daily 10–12, 2:15–6; in low season, Sun 2–5. Closed 15 Dec–1 Mar 💲 Moderate

The Northwest

Mortain
Le Village Enchanté
Take the model train around
this fairyland village, which
has the added attractions of
a park and a puppet theatre.
✉ Bellefontaine, 6km north of
Mortain, on D33 ☎ 02 33 59 01
93 🕐 Easter–end Sep, daily
10–7 💷 Moderate

St-Lô
Mini-Train des Marais
Red-capped drivers operate
the 'marshland mini-train',
pulling child-size wagons
around a 20cm-gauge track.
✉ Marchésieux, 6km east of
Periers, on D900 west of St-Lô
☎ 02 33 07 03 79 🕐 Jul–end
Aug, daily 2:30–dusk; Apr–Oct,
weekend only 💷 Cheap

Zoos and Aquariums

Central Normandy

Courseulles-sur-Mer
La Maison de la Mer
A journey through the sea
tunnel leads to views of
undersea life; the shell
collection is worth visiting.
✉ place du 6 Juin ☎ 02 31
37 92 58 🕐 May, Jun, Sep,
daily 9–1, 2–7; Jul, Aug, 9–7;
Oct–Apr, Tue–Sun 10–12, 2–6
💷 Moderate

Thury-Harcourt
Parc Zoologique de la Cabosse
Giraffes and other wild
animals wander through
10ha of wooded parkland.
Picnic area.
✉ Jurques, 20km west,
between Caen and Vire ☎ 02
31 77 80 58 🕐 Mid-Jan to end
Mar, Oct, Nov, daily 1:30–5:30;
Apr–Sep, 10–6 💷 Expensive

Trouville
Aquarium Écologique
No fewer than 60 tanks with
tropical and local fish, and
several varieties of shark.

Also creepy-crawlies and
reptiles, including Big Hug, a
6m python.
✉ Trouville beach ☎ 02 31 88
46 04 🕐 Easter–Jun, Sep, Oct,
daily 10–12, 2–7; Jul, Aug,
10–7:30, Nov–Easter, 2–6:30
💷 Moderate

The Northwest

Cherbourg
Cité de la Mer
Although mainly concerned
with man's adventures at
sea, among the attractions is
Europe's tallest cylindrical
aquarium. Known as the
Abyss, it offers a glimpse of
life below the surface of the
waters and was created by
the team responsible for
Nausicaa in Boulogne.
✉ Gare Maritime
Transatlantique ☎ 08 25 33 50
50 🕐 Feb–May mid-Sep–Dec
10–6; Jun–mid-Sep 9.30–7
💷 Expensive

Granville
L'Aquarium du Roc
Fish, shells and models;
same opening times and
charges as the nearby Féerie
des Coquillages (shell palace
and light show), and the
Palais Minéral et Jardin des
Papillons (minerals,
butterflies).
✉ boulevarde Vaufleury
☎ 02 33 50 19 83 🕐 Daily
9–7:30

Le Mont-St-Michel
Reptilarium du Mont-St-Michel
As well as the appeal of
crocodiles and iguanas,
pythons and boas, children
can explore tunnels, ladders, a
suspension bridge, pyramids,
towers and a maze. The
reptilarium is situated at
Beauvoir, on the mainland
opposite the mount.
✉ 62 route du Mont-St-Michel
☎ 02 33 68 11 18 🕐 Apr–end
Sep, daily 10–7; Oct–Mar, 2–6.
Closed weekends Jan
💷 Moderate

Tourist Trains
Children can ride through
several Norman resorts in
open wagons pulled at a
sedate pace by mini-
locomotives. Services
leave daily from: the
promenade Marcel Proust
in Cabourg (July and
August); the tourist office,
place St-Pierre, in Caen;
the town hall in Deauville;
the harbour car park in
Honfleur; the car park (La
Basilique) in Lisieux; the
beach at Trouville (daily
July and August,
weekends all year), and
from the Town Hall in
Viller-sur-Mer (July and
August).

Music and Theatre

Church Music
Keep an eye out for free or inexpensive concerts held at churches and cathedrals all over the region, with a particularly good choice in Rouen and Le Havre. These may include organ recitals, chamber groups or choral works; some of the smaller concerts take place at lunchtime. Events are usually publicised on the church noticeboards and at the local tourist office, and included on the listings page of the regional newspaper, *Paris-Normandie*.

Theatres and Concert Halls

Rouen

La Chapelle St Louis
This venue takes in touring national and international productions as well as showcasing student and fringe groups from the city.
⊠ Place de la Rougemare
☎ 02 35 98 45 05

Opera de Rouen
Major operatic and ballet productions, plus classical concerts, staged in a modern building overlooking the Seine.
⊠ quai de la Bourse ☎ 02 35 71 41 36

Théâtre Duchamp-Villon
A theatre space in the modern Centre St-Sever, in the southern suburbs. Productions include a season of modern ballet works.
⊠ 16 place de la Verrière, Centre St-Sever ☎ 02 35 18 28 10 ⬛ St-Sever ⬛ 7, 12, 33

The Northeast

Le Havre
Théâtre des Bains Douches
An interesting range of contemporary and experimental drama productions, as well as some fringe music events.
⊠ 22 rue Louis Lobasso
☎ 02 35 47 63 09

Théâtre de l'Hôtel de Ville
Popular productions and family shows in an annexe of the city's modern town hall, overlooking the central square's lawns and fountains.
⊠ place de l'Hôtel de Ville
☎ 02 35 19 45 74

Le Volcan
Dance, theatre and music form an adventurous programme of classical and modern work. Also lectures and changing exhibitions of photography.
⊠ Espace Oscar Niemeyer
☎ 02 35 19 10 10

Caen

Théâtre de Caen
Contemporary and traditional productions of music, opera, drama and dance.
⊠ 135 Boulevard du Maréchal Leclerc ☎ 02 31 30 76 20

Central Normandy

Évreux
La Théâtre d'Évreux – Scène Nationale
A lively programme of events including seasons of films in conjunction with the Cinéma Victor Hugo, plus a varied range of dance, music and drama productions.
⊠ place du Général de Gaulle
☎ 02 32 78 85 20

Lisieux
Théâtre de Lisieux
Interesting touring productions, including contemporary drama, at a very traditional venue.
⊠ 2 rue au Char ☎ 02 31 61 04 40

The Northwest

Cherbourg
Théâtre de Cherbourg
Set in an ornate building with a good café-restaurant attached; visiting orchestras, dance troupes and drama companies are included in a lively programme.
⊠ place Général-de-Gaulle
☎ 02 33 88 55 55

Coutances
Théâtre Municipal de Coutances
The varied programme includes classical and popular music, traditional and new drama, dance and comedy.
✉ Rue St-Maur ☎ 02 33 76 78 50

Granville
Archipel
Good and varied programme at this showcase theatre in the resort.
✉ Place Maréchal Foch ☎ 02 33 69 27 30

Live Music Venues

Rouen

La Bertelière
A piano bar on the eastern outskirts of Rouen, near the railway line.
✉ 164 le Mesnic Gremichon, St-Martin-du-Vivier ☎ 02 35 60 44 00 🕐 Closed Sat lunch, Sun eve

Le Saxo
Late night bar with regular jazz nights.
✉ 11 place Saint-Mar ☎ 02 35 98 24 92

The Northeast

Le Havre
L'Agora
Hip-hop and jazz nights at this firm favourite, which pulls in fans from across the region.
✉ Espace Oscar Niemeyer ☎ 02 32 74 09 70

Greenish Pub
Rock bands sometimes perform at this lively pub which has a regular happy hour (8 till 9).
✉ 35 rue Lemaistre ☎ 02 35 22 89 33

L'Hermès
New bands and retro gigs in this stalwart of the port music scene.
✉ 348 rue Aristide Briand ☎ 02 35 24 35 84

McDaid's
An Irish theme pub that sells Guinness, has a pool table, and features folk, rock and jazz bands on Thursdays and Fridays.
✉ 97 rue Paul Doumer ☎ 02 35 41 30 40 🕐 2PM–2AM

Caen

Café Mancel
Home to the Normandy Jazz Club and popular with lovers of classic swing, jazz and blues sounds.
✉ The Château ☎ 02 31 86 63 64

Texas Coyote
American-style bar with US rock music. Great if you're feeling homesick.
✉ 44 rue de Bras ☎ 02 31 38 83 13

Le Garsouille
Every Friday at 7:30pm, and on selected weeknights this is Caen's relaxed live music venue.
✉ 11 rue de Caumont ☎ 02 31 86 80 27

Hangar Café
The former Book Café is now an informal midweek music venue. Jazz nights once a month.
✉ 9 rue Fresnel ☎ 02 31 44 09 19 🕐 Tue–Fri

Oxygène B
Music venue for a predominantly student crowd. Lots of up and coming bands, and some themed evenings to attract a non-student audience.
✉ University Campus ☎ 02 31 56 60 95

The Northwest

Cherbourg
Casino Cherbourg
Disco, pub and restaurant on the quayside.
✉ quai Alexandre III ☎ 02 33 20 53 35

Cinemas
There's little problem finding mainstream movies, especially in Normandy's larger centres. Rouen has the multiscreen Gaumont (28 rue de la République) and UGC Les Clubs (75 rue de Général Leclerc), plus a cinema in the Centre St-Sever, across the river, and vintage and fringe films at Ariel (place Colbert) and Melville (12 rue St-Etienne). Le Havre has a choice including Eden, in the Espace Oscar Niemeyer, and there are several in Caen, including the Cinéma de Paris (12 avenue du 6 Juin), and Cinéma Lux (avenue Ste-Thérèse). Films marked 'VO' (Version Originale) are usually British or American, with the original soundtracks and French subtitles (soustitres).

Sport

Sport of Kings

Horse racing and horse breeding are big business in Normandy. Deauville's thoroughbred racehorse market turns over 150 million francs a year, and there are racecourses all over the region. Two organisations can provide details of courses and fixtures (which take place all through the year): the Fédération Régionale des Sociétés de Courses, BP 43, 14502 Vire (☎ 02 31 68 09 04); and the Ligue de Normandie des Sports Équestres, 10 place Demi-Lune, 14000 Caen (☎ 02 31 84 61 87).

Fishing and Watersports

There is plenty of opportunity for fishing in rivers, lakes and the sea (from pier or boat). Other popular sports are sailing, sand yachting or windsurfing. For information on clubs and organisations, contact the tourist office for each *département* (➤ 120). For details of sailing schools and yachting clubs, contact:

Centre Régional de Nautisme
✉ boulevard des Amiraux, Port de Hérel, 50400 Granville
☎ 02 33 91 22 60

Balleroy
Parc de Loisirs Cahagnolles
Leisure park has a 1.5ha lake for fishing, plus a campsite.
✉ Cahagnolles, 6km east of Balleroy ☎ 02 31 21 63 59

Cany-Barville
Lac de Caniel
From waterskiing to canoeing and pedalos to bungee-jumping, the 70ha site at Cany-Barville is a vast watersports and leisure complex with dry land activities for roller bladers and summer tobogganists alongside varied wet activities.
✉ Route du Lac 76450, Cany-Baraville (20km north-west of Fécamp on D925 ☎ 02 35 97 40 73

Lisieux
Canapvillle
Fly fishing on the Tourques at Canapville. Parages is the Pays d'Auge fishing association: Chambre de Commerce et d'Industrie du pays d'Auge, Lisieux.
✉ 8km west of Vimoutiers
☎ 02 31 48 52 06

Golf

The Golfing Passport is a scheme operated in Calvados that allows use of five green fees on five different courses (from a selection of six) on nine consecutive days. It must be booked in advance, though no payment is due until you arrive at the first golf course. Obtain the passport from:

Calvados Tourisme
✉ place du Canada, 14600 Caen
☎ 02 31 27 90 30

Caen
Golf de Caen 'Le Vallon'
A 27-hole course with a putting green, practice course, restaurant and clubhouse.
✉ 14112 Biéville-Beuville, 8km north of Caen ☎ 02 31 94 72 09

Cherbourg
La Glacerie
Six indoor and 12 outdoor practice greens, plus a 9-hole course. Golf practice schools Wednesday and Saturday.
✉ Domaines des Roches, La Glacerie, 4km southeast of Cherbourg, on D122 ☎ 02 33 44 45 48

Clécy
Golf de Clécy-Cantelou
Eighteen holes on the manor green, plus a putting green, clubhouse and restaurant.
✉ Manoir de Cantelou, 30km south of Caen on D562 ☎ 02 31 69 72 72

Deauville
New Golf de Deauville
Open daily (except Tuesday in winter), this 27-hole course also has a training green, golf shop and restaurant.

✉ 2km south of Deauville, off D278 ☎ 02 31 14 24 24

Dieppe
Golf de Dieppe
Established in 1897, this is one of Normandy's oldest golf courses; 18 holes.
✉ Western outskirts of Dieppe, off D75 ☎ 02 35 84 25 05

Golf de Garcelles
Two 9-hole courses, with a training bunker and putting green.
✉ route de Falaise, Garcelles-Secqueville, 6km south of Caen ☎ 02 31 39 09 09

Granville
Golf de Granville
27 holes along the seafront, a covered practice course, and two putting greens.
✉ 3km north of Granville at Bréville-sur-Mer, on D236/GR 223 ☎ 02 33 50 23 06

Le Havre
Golf du Havre
An 18-hole course where golfers have been swinging since the 1930s.
✉ Octeville-sur-Mer, 10km north of Le Havre ☎ 02 35 46 36 50

Rouen
Golf de Rouen
The city's 18-hole golf club, founded in 1911.
✉ Mont-St-Aignon, 5km north of Rouen on D43 ☎ 02 35 76 38 65

Go-karts
As with bowling, karting proves a popular weekend sport for French families. With indoor and outdoor circuits, this is a reliable all-weather activity.

Rouen
Rouen Espace Karting
350m indoor track, with 200–270cc adult go-karts.
✉ 149 chemin du Croisset ☎ 02 32 12 34 05

Dieppe
Euro Dieppe Karting
210m indoor track and a vast 700m outdoor circuit for adults and children.
✉ ZI Louis Delaporte, Rouxmesnil-Bouteilles (on the D154, leaving town) ✉ 02 35 06 13 13

Cycling
Cycles can be hired at several railway stations throughout the region and can be taken free of charge on some train services. The *département* tourist offices provide lists of cycle hire centres. For information on cycling and route maps, contact:

Fédération Française de Cyclotourisme (Ligue Basse-Normandie)
✉ 20 rue du Beau-Site, 14250 Tilly/Seulles ☎ 02 31 80 50 33

Fédération Française de Cyclotourisme (Ligue Haute-Normandie)
✉ 21 rue de l'Enseigne-Renaud, 76000 Rouen ☎ 02 35 89 45 06

Fédération Française de Cyclotourisme
✉ 8 rue Jean-Marie-Jégo, 75013 Paris ☎ 01 44 16 88 88

Treetop Walking
After centuries of enjoying woodland walkd from the forest floor, France has embraced tree-walking and 'acrobranching' activities, ranging from crossing between trees on suspended pathways to swinging Tarzan-style from the treetops.

Fécamp
Le Parc du Val aux Clerc
Fun for children and adults alike. Ladders and bridges – and full safety equipment – form a branch level circuit in an arc, which also hosts paintballing events.
✉ Ave du Maréchal de Lattre de Tassigny ☎ 02 35 10 84 83

Hiking and Walking
The Institut Géographique National (IGN) publishes large-scale maps showing long-distance paths (marked as GR, or Grandes Randonnés), several of which cross parts of Normandy. Guides that list paths are available from the Fédération Française de la Randonnée Pédestre, 64 rue de Gergovie, 75014 Paris (☎ 01 45 45 31 02); and, within Normandy, the Comité Départemental de Randonnée Pédestre de l'Orne, 2 rue René Fonck, 61000 Alençon (☎ 02 33 29 33 74); the Comité Départemental de Tourisme Pédestre du Calvados, 6 promenade de Madame-de-Sévigné, 14050 Caen (☎ 02 31 89 39 07); and the Comité Départemental de la Randonnée Pédestre de la Manche, Maison du Département, 50008 St-Lô (☎ 02 33 05 98 70).

What's On When

How to have fun
Besides the annual festivals, tourist offices have details of countless one-off celebrations and events in their own and nearby towns. In cities such as Caen and Rouen, glossy weekly listings magazines, with full details of plays, concerts, gigs and exhibitions, are available in popular bars, hotel foyers and on tourist office counters.

January–April
Apple markets, Parc Naturel Régional do Brotonne (ask at tourist offices for venues).

March
Tree Fair, Lisieux (first week).
Fair celebrating Mortagne-au-Perche's traditional blood-sausage (first week).
Scandinavian Film Festival, Rouen.

April
Rouen International Fair (first two weeks).

April–May
Street Theatre Festival, Fécamp.
Suisse Normande Marathon.

May
Jazz under the Apple Trees, Coutances.
Geranium Fair, Beuvron-en-Auge.
Spring Fair (religious and folk events), le Mont-St-Michel.
Seafarers' Pilgrimage, Honfleur.
Jeanne d'Arc Festival, Rouen.

June
Music Festival, venues throughout Orne.
Blessing of the Sea and Sea Festival, Le Havre.
Anniversary of Normandy Landings, D-Day Beaches (6 June).
Folklore Festival, Trouville.

June–October
Eure Summer Festival, venues throughout Eure.

July
Medieval Festival, Bayeux.
Pilgrimage across the beaches, le Mont-St-Michel.
Puppet Festival, Dives-sur-Mer.

July–August
Coutances Summer Festival.

August
Thoroughbred Yearling Auction and Polo Lancel Cup, Deauville.
Turkey Market, Lisieux.
Ancient Music Festival, Dieppe.
Cheese Fair, Livarot.
Les Traversées de Tatihou (traditional music and dancing), Île de Tatihou.

August–September
Presentation of stallions and horse teams of the national stud, St-Lô.
Music Festival Orne.
Donkey racing at Trouville.

September
Sea Festival (La Mer en Fête), Le Havre.
Horse racing, parade and presentation of studs, le Pin-au-Haras.
Caen International Fair.
American Film Festival, Deauville.
Ancient Ste-Croix Fair, Lessay.
International Mushroom Fair, Bellême.

October
Horse Week, locations throughout Calvados.
Cider Market and Festival, Beuvron-en-Auge.
Shrimp Festival, Honfleur.
International Flower Show, Lisieux.
Jacques Vabre Transatlantic Race, Le Havre.

November
Horse jumping (Jump'Orne), Alençon.
Apple Festival, Le Havre.

December
Turkey Fair, Sées.

Practical Matters

Above: *the best way to travel in rural Normandy*
Right: *a sign of accommodation with character*

TIME DIFFERENCES

GMT
12 noon

France
1PM

Germany
1PM

USA (NY)
7AM

Netherlands
1PM

Spain
1PM

BEFORE YOU GO

WHAT YOU NEED

● Required ○ Suggested ▲ Not required	Some countries require a passport to remain valid for a minimum period (usually at least six months) beyond the date of entry – contact their consulate or embassy or your travel agent for details.	UK	Germany	USA	Netherlands	Spain
Passport/National Identity Card		●	●	●	●	●
Visa (Regulations can change – check before your journey)		▲	▲	▲	▲	▲
Onward or Return Ticket		▲	▲	▲	▲	▲
Health Inoculations		▲	▲	▲	▲	▲
Health Documentation (➤ 123, Health)		●	●	●	●	●
Travel Insurance		○	○	○	○	○
Driving Licence (national)		●	●	●	●	●
Car Insurance Certificate (if own car)		●	●	●	●	●
Car Registration Document (if own car)		●	●	●	●	●

WHEN TO GO

Caen

High season

Low season

7°C	8°C	12°C	13°C	17°C	20°C	22°C	22°C	20°C	15°C	11°C	8°C
JAN	FEB	MAR	APR	MAY	JUN	JUL	AUG	SEP	OCT	NOV	DEC

Very wet ▪ Wet ▪ Cloud ▪ Sun ▪ Showers

TOURIST OFFICES

In the UK
French Tourist Office
178 Piccadilly
London W1V 0AL
☎ 020 7399 3500
(recorded information)
fax 020 493 6594

Normandy Tourist Board
The Old Bakery
Bath Hill
Keynsham
Bristol BS18 1HG
☎ 0117 986 0386
fax 0117 986 0379

In the USA
French Government
Tourist Office
444 Madison Avenue
16th floor
New York NY 10022
☎ 212/838 7800
fax 212/838 7855

POLICE 17

FIRE 18

AMBULANCE 15

SOS TRAVELLERS 04 91 62 12 80

WHEN YOU ARE THERE

ARRIVING

Airports at Caen, Cherbourg, Deauville, Le Havre and Rouen take international flights. Ferries travel from the UK to Cherbourg, Ouistreham, Le Havre and Dieppe, with high-speed services to Cherbourg and Ouistreham in summer. There are also services from Ireland to Cherbourg and Le Havre. The junction of the A28 and A16 roads at Abbeville provides a direct link between Normandy and the Eurotunnel at Calais.

Rouen Airport	Journey Times	
Kilometres to city centre	🚋	N/A
	🚌	N/A
7 kilometres	🚗	10 minutes

MONEY

The euro is the official currency of France. Euro banknotes and coins were introduced in January 2002. Banknotes are in denominations of 5, 10, 20, 50, 100, 200 and 500 euros and coins are in denominations of 1, 2, 5, 10, 20 and 50 cents, and 1 and 2 euros. Euro traveller's cheques are widely accepted, as are major credit cards. Credit and debit cards can also be used for withdrawing euro notes from cashpoint machines. Cashpoints are widely accessible throughout the city. France's former currency, the French franc, went out of circulation in early 2002.

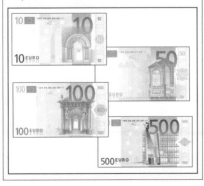

TIME

France is one hour ahead of Greenwich Mean Time (GMT+1), but from late March, when clocks are put forward one hour, until late October French summer time (GMT+2) operates.

CUSTOMS

YES

Goods Obtained Duty Free Inside the EU or Goods Bought Outside the EU (Limits):
Alcohol over 22% vol: 1L *or*
Alcohol not over 22% vol: 2L
Still table wine: 2L
Cigarettes: 200 *or*
Cigars: 50 *or*
Tobacco: 250g
Perfume: 60ml
Toilet water: 250ml
Goods Bought Duty and Tax Paid Inside the EU (Guidance Levels):
Alcohol over 22% vol: 10L
Alcohol not over 22% vol: 20L
Wine: 90L (max 60L sparkling)
Beer: 110L
Cigarettes: 3200 *or*
Cigars: 200 *or*
Tobacco: 3kg
Perfume: no limit
Toilet water: no limit
You must be 17 or over to benefit from the alcohol and tobacco allowances.

NO

Drugs, firearms, ammunition, offensive weapons, obscene material, unlicensed animals.

EMBASSIES AND CONSULATES

UK
01 42 66 91 42
(Paris Embassy)
01 42 66 38 10
(Paris consulate)

Germany
01 42 99 78 00
(Paris Embassy)

USA
01 43 12 22 22
(Paris Embassy)

Netherlands
01 40 62 33 00
(Paris Embassy)

Spain
01 44 43 18 18
(Paris Embassy)
01 47 66 03 32
(Paris Consulate)

WHEN YOU ARE THERE

TOURIST OFFICES

Comité Régional du Tourisme de Normandie
● 14 rue Charles Corbeau
27000 Évreux
☎ 02 32 33 79 00

Departmental Tourist Offices
● Comité Départemental de Tourisme du Calvados
8 rue Renoir
14054 Caen
☎ 02 31 27 90 30

● Comité Départemental de Tourisme de l'Eure
3 rue Commandant Letellier
BP 367
27003 Évreux
☎ 02 32 62 04 27

● Comité Départemental de Tourisme d'Eure-et-Loir
10 rue du Dr Maunoury
BP 67
28002 Chartres cedex
☎ 02 37 84 01 00

● Comité Départemental de Tourisme de la Manche
route de Villedieu
50008 St-Lô
☎ 02 33 05 98 70

● Comité Départemental de Tourisme de l'Orne
88 rue St-Blaise
BP 50
61002 Alençon
☎ 02 33 28 88 71

● Comité Départemental de Tourisme de Seine-Maritime
6 rue Couronné
BP 60
76420 Bihorel-les-Rouen
☎ 02 35 12 10 10

NATIONAL HOLIDAYS

J	F	M	A	M	J	J	A	S	O	N	D
1		(2)	(2)	3(2)	(2)	1	1			2	1

1 Jan	New Year's Day
Mar/Apr	Easter Sunday and Monday
1 May	Labour Day
8 May	VE Day
May	Ascension Day
May/Jun	Whit Sunday and Monday
14 Jul	Bastille Day
15 Aug	Assumption Day
1 Nov	All Saints' Day
11 Nov	Remembrance Day
25 Dec	Christmas Day

OPENING HOURS

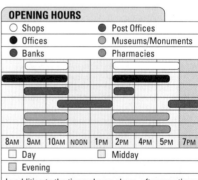

○ Shops	● Post Offices
● Offices	○ Museums/Monuments
● Banks	○ Pharmacies

| 8AM | 9AM | 10AM | NOON | 1PM | 2PM | 4PM | 5PM | 7PM |

□ Day   □ Midday
▨ Evening

In addition to the times shown above, afternoon times of shops in summer can extend in the most popular centres. Most shops close Sunday and many on Monday. Small food shops open from 7AM and may open Sunday morning. Large department stores do not close for lunch and hypermarkets open 10AM to 9 or 10PM, but may shut Monday morning. Banks are closed Sunday as well as Saturday or Monday. Museums and monuments have extended summer hours. Many close one day a week: either Monday (municipal ones) or Tuesday (national ones).

**DRIVE ON THE
RIGHT**

**TOILETS
FREE**

PUBLIC TRANSPORT

 Internal Flights Air Atlantique operates daily flights from Paris (Roissy-Charles de Gaulle and Orly) to Cherbourg (just under an hour).

 Trains Main lines connect Paris with Rouen, Le Havre, Dieppe, Caen, Cherbourg and Granville. Within Normandy there is a wide rail network linking all the main centres and many smaller towns. Free timetables are available from tourist offices for regional transport (train lines and inter-centre buses) in Haute-Normandie and Basse-Normandie.

 Buses Most sizeable towns have a bus station (*gare routière*). Some lines operate in conjunction with SNCF trains; other, local services link smaller towns and villages, and Bus verts du Calvados operate some of the longer rural lines. Apart from the regional transport lines (see Trains), timetables are quite difficult to find outside major centres such as Rouen and Caen, but times are often posted on the bus stops themselves.

 Boats and Ferries Émeraude Lines run ferries to Jersey, with connections to Guernsey and Sark from Granville (☎ 02 33 50 16 36) and Carteret (☎ 02 33 52 61 39). Boats go to the Îles Chausey from Granville and to the Île Tatihou from St-Vaast-la-Hougue.

 Urban Transport Urban bus routes operate in larger cities. Rouen has installed a Métrobus that links both banks of the Seine and extends south into the suburbs. A booklet giving details of the Métrobus is available free from the Rouen tourist office, 25 place de la Cathédrale (☎ 02 32 08 32 40).

CAR RENTAL

 All large towns have car-rental agencies at their airports and railway stations. Car hire is expensive, but airlines and tour operators offer fly-drive and French Railways (SNCF) train-car packages, often more economical than hiring locally.

TAXIS

 Taxis are a costlier option than public transport. They pick up at taxi ranks (*stations de taxi*) found at railway stations and airports. Hotels and restaurants can usually give a taxi call number. Check the taxi has a meter; there is a pick-up charge plus a rate per minute.

DRIVING

 Speed limits on toll motorways (autoroutes): **130kph (110kph when wet)**; non-toll motorways and dual carriageways: **110kph (100kph when wet)**. In fog (visibility less than 50m): **50kph** all roads

 Speed limits on country roads: **90kph (80kph when wet)**

 Speed limits on urban roads: **50kph** (limit starts at town sign)

 Must be worn in front seats at all times and in rear seats where fitted.

 Random breath-testing. Never drive under the influence of alcohol.

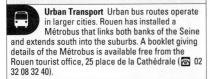 Petrol (*essence*) including unleaded (*sans plomb*), and diesel (*gasoil*) is widely available. Petrol stations are numerous along main roads but rarer in rural areas. Some on minor roads are closed on Sundays. Maps showing petrol stations are available from main tourist offices.

 A red warning triangle must be carried if your car has no hazard warning lights. Place the triangle 30m behind the car in the event of an accident or breakdown. On motorways ring from emergency phones (every 2km) to contact the breakdown service. Off motorways, police will advise on local breakdown services.

PERSONAL SAFETY

The *Police Municipale* (blue uniforms) carry out police duties in cities and towns. The *Gendarmes* (blue trousers, black jackets, white belts), the national police force, cover the countryside and smaller places. The *CRS* deal with emergencies and also look after safety on beaches.

To avoid danger or theft:
• Do not use unmanned roadside rest areas at night.
• Cars, especially foreign cars, should be secured.
• In crowded places, beware of pickpockets.

Police assistance:
☎ **17**
from any call box

TELEPHONES

Telephone numbers in France comprise ten digits; the first two for Normandy numbers are 02 (omit 0 if dialling from the UK). Many public phones use pre-

paid cards (*télécartes*); these can be bought at post offices, *bureaux de tabac* and branches of France Télécom. They come in units of 50 or 120.

International Dialling Codes	
From France:	
UK:	**00 44**
Germany:	**00 49**
USA & Canada:	**00 1**
Netherlands:	**00 31**
Spain:	**00 34**

POST

The PTT (*Postes et Télécommunications*) deals with mail and telephone services. Outside main centres, post offices open shorter hours and may close 12–2. Letter boxes are yellow. Open: 8AM–7PM (till 12 Sat). Closed: Sun. Main post office in Rouen: 45 rue Jeanne d'Arc (☎ 02 32 76 66 20).

ELECTRICITY

The French power supply is: 220 volts
Type of socket:

 Round two-hole sockets taking two-round-pin (or occasionally three-round-pin) plugs. British visitors should bring an adaptor; US visitors a voltage transformer.

TIPS/GRATUITIES

Yes ✓ No ✗		
Restaurants (service incl., tip optional)	✗	
Cafés/Bar (service incl., tip optional)	✗	
Hotels (service incl., tip optional	✗	
Hairdressers	✓	€1
Taxis	✓	€1
Tour guides	✓	€1
Cinema usherettes	✓	€1
Cloakroom attendants	✓	change
Toilet attendants	✓	change

What to photograph: the coast, with its broad sands and beautiful light; rural villages and timber-framed houses; abbey and château ruins; le Mont-St-Michel.

Restrictions: some museums will allow you to photograph inside. In churches with frescos and icons, prior permission is required for flashlight.

Where to buy film: the most popular brands and types of film can be bought from shops and photo laboratories. Film development is quite expensive.

HEALTH

Insurance
Nationals of EU and certain other countries can get medical treatment in France at reduced cost on production of a qualifying form (Form E111 for Britons), although private medical insurance is still advised and is essential for all other visitors.

Dental Services
As for general medical treatment (see above, **Insurance**), nationals of EU countries can obtain dental treatment at reduced cost. About 70 per cent of a dentist's standard fee can be refunded. Private medical insurance is still advisable for all.

Sun Advice
The sunniest (and hottest) months are July and August, but the good weather can start in June and continue to October. Although the weather is mild, take care on the beach and when walking, when you are more likely to get burnt. Drink plenty of fluids, wear a hat and apply sunscreen.

Drugs
Pharmacies – recognised by their green cross sign – have qualified staff able to offer medical advice, provide first aid, and prescribe and provide a wide range of drugs, though some are available by prescription (*ordonnance*) only.

Safe Water
It is safe to drink tap water served in hotels and restaurants, but never drink from a tap marked *eau non potable* (not drinking water). Many prefer the taste of bottled water, which is cheap and widely available.

CONCESSIONS

Students/Youths A youth card (*Carte Jeune*), available to those under 26, entitles holders to various discounts on public transport, museum admissions, entertainments, shopping and other facilities (including meals in university canteens): ask at tourist offices and post offices for details.

Senior Citizens A number of tour companies offer special arrangements for senior citizens; for further information contact the French Tourist Office (► 118, **Tourist Offices**). Senior citizens are eligible for reduced or free entrance to sights (aged 60 and over), and discounts on public transport (aged 65 and over).

CLOTHING SIZES

France	UK	Rest of Europe	USA	
46	36	46	36	Suits
48	38	48	38	
50	40	50	40	
52	42	52	42	
54	44	54	44	
56	46	56	46	
41	7	41	8	Shoes
42	7.5	42	8.5	
43	8.5	43	9.5	
44	9.5	44	10.5	
45	10.5	45	11.5	
46	11	46	12	
37	14.5	37	14.5	Shirts
38	15	38	15	
39/40	15.5	39/40	15.5	
41	16	41	16	
42	16.5	42	16.5	
43	17	43	17	
36	8	34	6	Dresses
38	10	36	8	
40	12	38	10	
42	14	40	12	
44	16	42	14	
46	18	44	16	
38	4.5	38	6	Shoes
38	5	38	6.5	
39	5.5	39	7	
39	6	39	7.5	
40	6.5	40	8	
41	7	41	8.5	

WHEN DEPARTING

- Remember to contact the airport on the day before leaving to ensure the flight details are unchanged.
- If travelling by ferry you must check in no later than the time specified on your ticket.
- Check the duty-free limits of the country you are entering before departure.

LANGUAGE

French is the native language. English is spoken widely, especially by those involved in the tourist trade and working in the larger and most popular centres; in smaller, rural places fewer people speak English. In any case, attempts to speak French, or at least to greet others in French, will be much appreciated. Below is a list of helpful words. More extensive coverage can be found in the AA's *Essential French Phrase Book*.

	hotel	*l'hôtel*	rate	*le tarif*	
	guest house	*chambre d'hôte*	breakfast	*le petit déjeuner*	
	room	*la chambre*	toilet	*les toilettes*	
	single room	*une personne*	bathroom	*la salle de bain*	
	double room	*deux personnes*	shower	*la douche*	
	per person	*par personne*	balcony	*le balcon*	
	per room	*par chambre*	key	*la clef/clé*	
	one/two nights	*une/deux nuits*	chambermaid	*femme*	
	reservation	*la réservation*		*de chambre*	

	bank	*la banque*	banknote	*le billet*	
	exchange office	*le bureau de change*	coin	*la pièce*	
			credit card	*la carte de crédit*	
	post office	*la poste*		*le chèque de*	
	cashier	*le caissier*	travellers' cheque	*voyage*	
	foreign exchange	*le change extérieur*	exchange rate	*le taux de change*	
	English pound	*la livre sterling*			

	restaurant	*la restaurant*	starter	*le hors d'œuvre*	
	café	*le café*	main course	*le plat principal*	
	table	*la table*	dish of the day	*le plat du jour*	
	menu	*le menu*	dessert	*le dessert*	
	set menu	*le menu du jour*	drink	*la boisson*	
	wine list	*la carte des vins*	waiter	*le garçon*	
	lunch	*le déjeuner*	waitress	*la serveuse*	
	dinner	*le dîner*	the bill	*l'addition*	

	aeroplane	*l'avion*	single/return	*simple/retour*	
	airport	*l'aéroport*	ticket office	*le guichet*	
	train	*le train*	timetable	*l'horaire*	
	train station	*la gare*	seat	*la place*	
	bus	*l'autobus*	first class	*première classe*	
	bus station	*la gare routière*	second class	*seconde classe*	
	ferry/boat	*le bateau*	non-smoking	*non-fumeurs*	
	port	*le port*	reserved	*réservé*	
	ticket	*le billet*	window	*la fenêtre*	

	yes	*oui*	today	*aujourd'hui*	
	no	*non*	tomorrow	*demain*	
	please	*s'il vous plaît*	yesterday	*hier*	
	thank you	*merci*	how much?	*combien?*	
	hello	*bonjour*	expensive	*cher*	
	goodbye	*au revoir*	open	*ouvert*	
	goodnight	*bonsoir*	closed	*fermé*	
	sorry	*pardon*	you're welcome	*de rien*	
	excuse me	*excusez-moi*	okay	*d'accord*	
	help!	*au secours!*	I don't know	*je ne sais pas*	

INDEX

The Automobile Association would like to thank the following photographers and libraries for their
assistance in the preparation of this book: BRIDGEMAN ART LIBRARY, LONDON 14b, Self
Portrait, 1917 by Claude Monet (1840–1926) Musée D'Orsay, Paris, France/Bridgeman Art Gallery,
London/New York, 22b Music at the Customs House at Le Havre by Raoul Dufy (1877–1953)
Musée Des Beaux-Arts André Malraux, Le Havre/Giraudon/Bridgeman Art Library, London;
ROBERT HARDING PICTURE LIBRARY 5b; HULTON GETTY 11b; PICTURES COLOUR LIBRARY
28/29; POWERSTOCK/ZEFA 24/25; SPECTRUM COLOUR LIBRARY 10b, 58, 63b

The remaining photographs are held in the Association's own library (AA PHOTO LIBRARY)
and were taken by Rob Moore, with the exception of pages 117b, 122a by J Edmanson; 122b
by Paul Kenward; 2, 122c by Tony Oliver; F/cover c (Gros Horloge), e (cemetery), f (Bayeux
Cathedral), h (lady), 1, 7b, 8c, 15a, 16a, 17a, 17b, 18a, 19a, 19b, 20a, 20b, 21a, 21b, 22a, 23a,
24a, 25a, 26a, 26b, 27b, 28a, 37, 40b, 43b, 46b, 48, 55b, 57b, 62, 65a, 68b, 72b, 75b, 81, 82,
83, 84, 86, 88, 117a by Clive Sawyer; 9c, 89 by Barrie Smith and F/cover (a) and B/cover (Mont St
Michel) by Rick Strange.

Author's Acknowledgements
Nia Williams wishes to thank Tony Evans, Dr Neil Kenny, and Stephen Rodgers and Lucy Walker
of the Normandy Tourist Board for all their help and advice.

Dear Essential Traveller

Your comments, opinions and recommendations are very important to us. So please help us to improve our travel guides by taking a few minutes to complete this simple questionnaire.

You do not need a stamp (unless posted outside the UK). If you do not want to cut this page from your guide, then photocopy it or write your answers on a plain sheet of paper.

Send to: **The Editor, AA World Travel Guides, FREEPOST SCE 4598, Basingstoke RG21 4GY.**

Your recommendations...

We always encourage readers' recommendations for restaurants, nightlife or shopping – if your recommendation is used in the next edition of the guide, we will send you a *FREE* AA *Essential* Guide of your choice. Please state below the establishment name, location and your reasons for recommending it.

_____

_____

_____

_____

Please send me **AA *Essential*** _____

About this guide...

Which title did you buy?
  AA *Essential* _____

Where did you buy it? _____

When? m m / y y

Why did you choose an AA *Essential* Guide? _____

_____

_____

_____

_____

Did this guide meet your expectations?
  Exceeded ☐ Met all ☐ Met most ☐ Fell below ☐
  Please give your reasons _____

_____

_____

_____

continued on next page...

Were there any aspects of this guide that you particularly liked? _____
_____
_____

Is there anything we could have done better? _____
_____
_____

About you...

Name (*Mr/Mrs/Ms*) _____
    Address _____
_____
_____ Postcode _____
    Daytime tel nos _____

Please only give us your mobile phone number if you wish to hear from us
about other products and services from the AA and partners by text or mms.

Which age group are you in?
    Under 25 ☐ 25–34 ☐ 35–44 ☐ 45–54 ☐ 55–64 ☐ 65+ ☐

How many trips do you make a year?
    Less than one ☐ One ☐ Two ☐ Three or more ☐

Are you an AA member? Yes ☐ No ☐

About your trip...

When did you book? m m / y y   When did you travel? m m / y y
How long did you stay? _____
Was it for business or leisure? _____
Did you buy any other travel guides for your trip?
    If yes, which ones? _____

Thank you for taking the time to complete this questionnaire. Please send it to us as soon as
possible, and remember, you do not need a stamp (*unless posted outside the UK*).

Happy Holidays!

The information we hold about you will be used to provide the products and services requested
and for identification, account administration, analysis, and fraud/loss prevention purposes. More
details about how that information is used is in our privacy statement, which you'll find under the
heading "Personal Information" in our terms and conditions and on our website: www.theAA.com.
Copies are also available from us by post, by contacting the Data Protection Manager at AA,
Southwood East, Apollo Rise, Farnborough, Hampshire GU14 OJW.

We may want to contact you about other products and services provided by us, or our partners (by
mail, telephone) but please tick the box if you DO NOT wish to hear about such products and
services from us by mail or telephone. ☐

The Atlas

Acknowledgements
All pictures are from AA World Travel Library with contributions from the following photographers:
Ian Dawson: the seaside town of Barfleur; car in Deauville; artist on Barneville-Careret beach; horse and cart at Barfleur; Mont St Michel; promenading in Deauville
Clive Sawyer: the gardens of Monet's house in Giverny
Rob Moore: reflection of the spire of Rouen Cathedral

The Automobile Association
www.theAA.com
The Automobile Association's website offers comprehensive and up-to-the-minute information covering AA-approved hotels, guest houses and B&Bs, restaurants and pubs in the UK; airport parking, insurance, European breakdown cover, European motoring advice, a ferry planner, European route planner, overseas fuel prices, a bookshop and much more.

The Foreign and Commonwealth Office
Country advice, traveller's tips, before you go information, checklists and more.
www.fco.gov.uk

French National Tourist Office
www.franceguide.com

GENERAL
UK Passport Service
www.ukpa.gov.uk

Health Advice for Travellers
www.doh.gov.uk/traveladvice

UK Travel Insurance Directory
www.uktravelinsurancedirectory.co.uk

BBC – Holiday
www.bbc.co.uk/holiday

The Full Universal Currency Converter
www.xe.com/ucc/full.shtml

Flying with Kids
www.flyingwithkids.com

Up-to-date information on places, prices and holidays throughout Normandy.
www.Normandy-tourism.org

Normandy is divided into five administrative départements and two of them have good English language websites with information and links to local sites:
Eure: www.cdt-eure.fr
Manche: www.manchetourisme.com

The following sites, in French only, are useful for links and brochure ordering service:
Calvados: www.calvados-tourisme.com
Orne: www.ornetourisme.com
Seine Maritime: www.seine-maritime-tourisme.com

For current listings of entertainment, exhibitions and events, as well as local detail, town and city websites are invaluable.
Bayeux: www.bayeux-tourism.com
Caen: www.ville-caen.fr/tourisme
Cherbourg: www.ville-cherbourg.fr/Anglais
Rouen: www.rouentourisme.com

The official site of the D-Day and Battle of Normandy memorials, events and sites.
www.normandiememoire.com

GETTING AROUND
US and UK sites for information on rail travel to, from and around the region. Information on regional timetables passes and buying tickets on line. www.raileurope.com
www.raileurope.co.uk

ACCOMMODATION
Tourist office websites can help with booking city centre and resort accommodation. However, independent travellers should check out the following sites.

For self-catering accommodation meeting rigidly verified standards, the Gîtes de France logo is the national standard. Converted barns, farmhouses, watermills and country cottages across the region are listed online as is a superb selected of registered B&B Chambre d'Hôtes. Easy reservations facility. www.gites-de-france.fr

The national federation of independent family run hotels, inns and restaurants has an easy to use and well illustrated website for selecting and booking accommodation and meals. www.logisdefrance.com

FLIGHTS AND INFORMATION
www.cheapflights.co.uk
www.thisistravel.co.uk
www.ba.com
www.worldairportguide.com

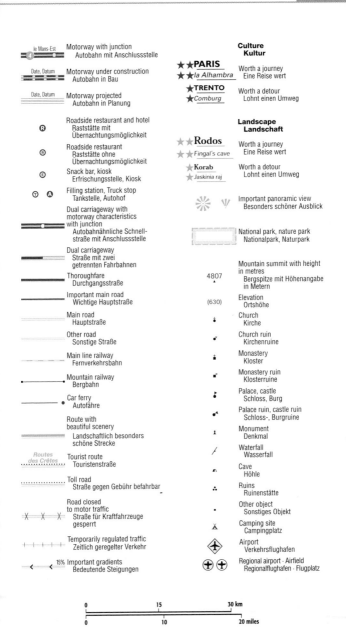

Motorway with junction
Autobahn mit Anschlussstelle
le Mans-Est

Motorway under construction
Autobahn in Bau
Date, Datum

Motorway projected
Autobahn in Planung
Date, Datum

Roadside restaurant and hotel
Raststätte mit
Übernachtungsmöglichkeit
ⓡ

Roadside restaurant
Raststätte ohne
Übernachtungsmöglichkeit
ⓡ

Snack bar, kiosk
Erfrischungsstelle, Kiosk
ⓔ

Filling station, Truck stop
Tankstelle, Autohof
ⓣ Ⓐ

**Dual carriageway with
motorway characteristics
with junction**
Autobahnähnliche Schnell-
straße mit Anschlussstelle

Dual carriageway
Straße mit zwei
getrennten Fahrbahnen

Thoroughfare
Durchgangsstraße

Important main road
Wichtige Hauptstraße

Main road
Hauptstraße

Other road
Sonstige Straße

Main line railway
Fernverkehrsbahn

Mountain railway
Bergbahn

Car ferry
Autofähre

**Route with
beautiful scenery**
Landschaftlich besonders
schöne Strecke

Tourist route
Touristenstraße
*Routes
des Crêtes*

Toll road
Straße gegen Gebühr befahrbar

**Road closed
to motor traffic**
Straße für Kraftfahrzeuge
gesperrt
X — X — X

Temporarily regulated traffic
Zeitlich geregelter Verkehr

Important gradients
Bedeutende Steigungen
◂— ◂ 15%

Culture
Kultur

★ ★**PARIS**
★ ★*la Alhambra*
Worth a journey
Eine Reise wert

★**TRENTO**
★*Comburg*
Worth a detour
Lohnt einen Umweg

Landscape
Landschaft

★ ★**Rodos**
★ ★*Fingal's cave*
Worth a journey
Eine Reise wert

★**Korab**
★*Jaskinia raj*
Worth a detour
Lohnt einen Umweg

☀ ⩔ **Important panoramic view**
Besonders schöner Ausblick

National park, nature park
Nationalpark, Naturpark

**Mountain summit with height
in metres**
Bergspitze mit Höhenangabe
in Metern
4807
▲

Elevation
Ortshöhe
(630)

Church
Kirche
⸸

Church ruin
Kirchenruine
⸕

Monastery
Kloster
⸸

Monastery ruin
Klosterruine
⸕

Palace, castle
Schloss, Burg

Palace ruin, castle ruin
Schloss-, Burgruine

Monument
Denkmal

Waterfall
Wasserfall
⟋

Cave
Höhle

Ruins
Ruinenstätte

Other object
Sonstiges Objekt

Camping site
Campingplatz
Ⅹ

✈ **Airport**
Verkehrsflughafen

⊕ ⊕ **Regional airport · Airfield**
Regionalflughafen · Flugplatz

0		15		30 km
0		10		20 miles

Maps © Mairs Geographischer Verlag / Falk Verlag, 73751 Ostfildern

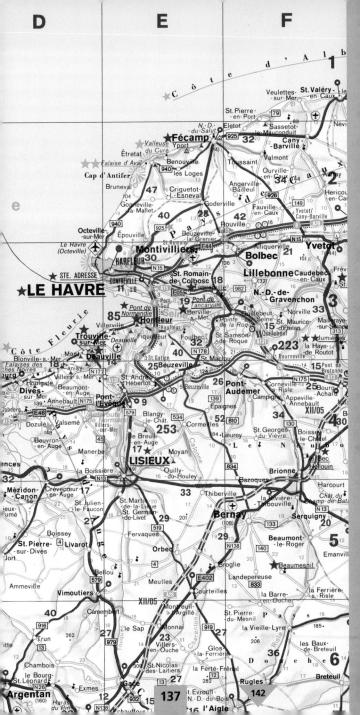

Top row (coordinates D E F, row 1):
Côte d'Albâtre
Veulettes-sur-Mer
St. Valéry-en-Caux
St. Pierre-en-Port
Eletot
79
83
Sassetot-le-Mauconduit
N.-D.-du-Salut
FÉCAMP
925
32
Cany-Barville
Yport

Row 2:
Valleuse du Curé
Étretat
Falaise d'Aval
Benouville
Toussaint
Valmont
Les Loges
940
Cap d'Antifer
Ourville-en-Caux
34
Bruneval
Criquetot-l'Esneval
104
Angerville-Bailleul
47
Gonneville-la-Mallet
Goderville
926
Héricou-en-Ca
149
Fauville-en-Caux
Yvetot/Cany-Barville
Octeville-sur-Mer
40
Épouville
925
25
Rouville
42
Pays
16
Beuzeville-bolbec
N 15
Le Havre (Octeville)
HARFLEUR
Montivilliers
30
E 44
Alliquerville
21
Bolbec
Yvetot
151

Row 3:
STE. ADRESSE
CONTREVILLE L'O.
11
St. Romain-de-Colbosc
18
982
N.-D.-de-Gravenchon
LE HAVRE
Lillebonne
Caudebec-en-Caux
E 05
Port-Sud
19
Pont de Tancarville
Berville-sur-Mer
Norville
33
Pont de Normandie
Honfleur
Quillebeuf
St. Maurice-d'Etelan
Maillerave-sur-Seine
85
Villerville
Honfleur
Pointe de la Roque
15
Quilleboeuf
313
Foulbec
St. Samson-de-la-Roque
A 131
Jumièges

Row 4:
Côte Fleurie
Trouville-sur-Mer
Deauville
Criqueboeuf
32
223
la Haye-de-Routot
Blonville-s.-Mer
Mont
St. Gatien
40
N 178
St. Maclou
15
Pont de Brotonne
18
Villers-s.-Mer
25
Beuzeville
124
Bourneville
N 175
Bourg-Achard
Houlgate
St. André-d'Hébertot
26
Pont-Audemer
Corneville-sur-Risle
25
Dives-sur-Mer
Beaumont-en-Auge
139
Beuzeville
Campigny
Appeville-Annebault
XII/05
Cabourg
Annebault
N 175
Pont-l'Évêque
9
Epaignes
130
Boissey-le-Châtel
4
30
E 46
Valsemé
579
Blangy-le-Chât.
534
52
810
Lieurey
St. Georges-du-Vièvre
Dozulé
148
Villers-sur-Mer
253
Cormeilles
84
Le Neubourg
45
Beuvron-en-Auge
Manerbe
Le Breuil-en-Auge
Moyan
834
Brionne
Le Bec-Hellouin
32
la Boissière
LISIEUX
Quilly-du-Houley
16
Bazoques
Harcourt

Lower rows:
Mézidon-Canon
Crèvecœur-en-Auge
17
St. Julien-le-Faucon
St. Martin-de-la-Lieue
33
Thiberville
la Rivière-Thibouville
Serquigny
20
St. Germain-de-Livet
20l
27
519
29
Bernay
(108)
133
N 13
Boissey
Fervaques
4
Livarot
23
Orbec
29
N 138
Beaumont-le-Roger
140
St. Pierre-sur-Dives
579
Bellou
4
Broglie
Landepereuse
833
Beaumesnil
Ammeville
Meulles
E 402
Courteilles
la Barre-en-Ouche
la Ferrière-s.-Risle
Vimoutiers
XII/05
Montreuil-l'Argillé
St. Pierre-du-Mesnil
Pays
40
Camembert
le Sap
Monnai
919
la Vieille-Lyre
185
916
262
27
979
23
Villers-en-Ouche
Glos-la-Ferrière
206
les Baux-de-Breteuil
36
Trun
13
St. Nicolas-des-Laitiers
la Ferté-Frênel
12
Rugles
Breteuil
Chambois
Dives
Gacé
27
St. Evroult-N.-D.-du-Bois
282
St. Léonard
Exmes
13
12
ARGENTAN
(160)
932
C
16
l'Aigle
N 138
Haras du Pin

137   142

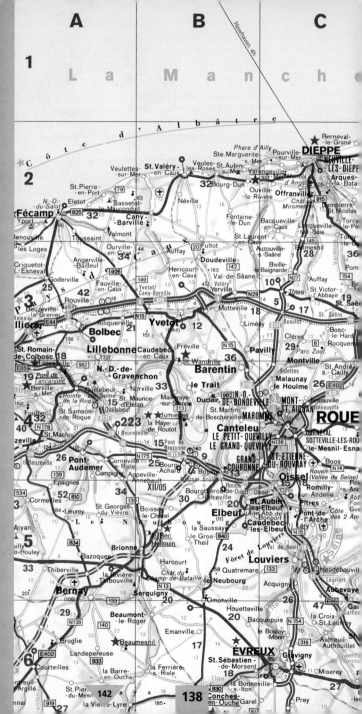

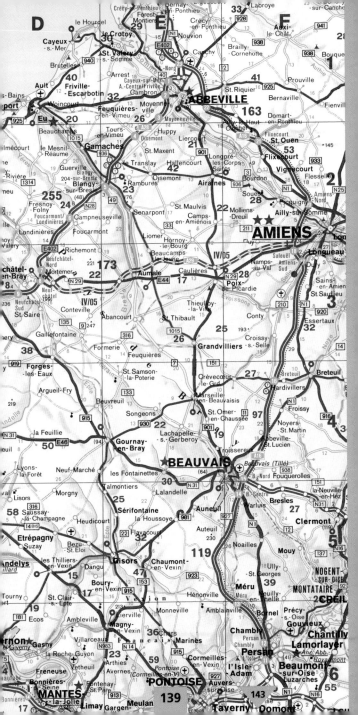

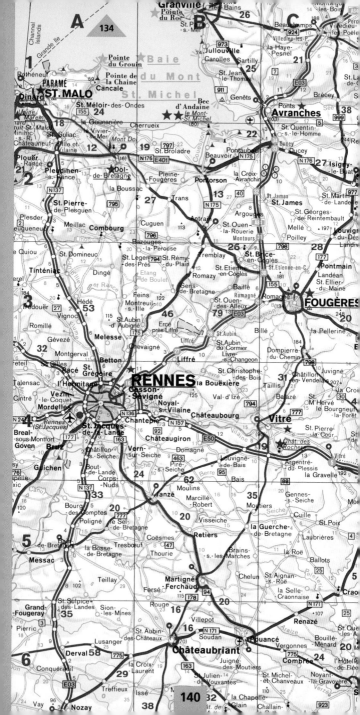

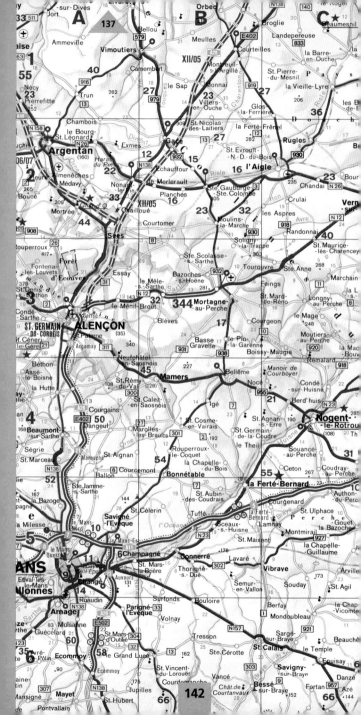

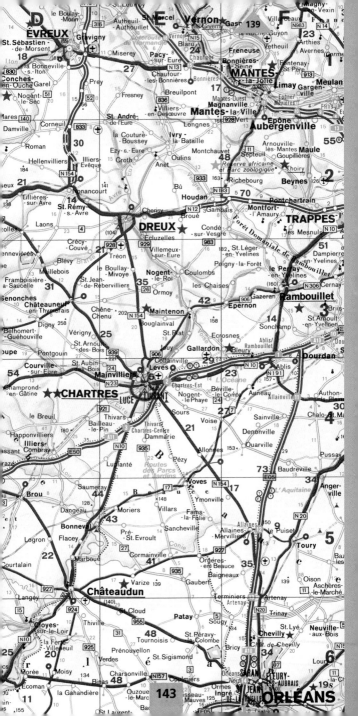

143

Sight Locator Index

This index relates to the atlas section on pages 134–143. We have given map references to the main sights of interest in the book. Some sights in the index may not be plotted on the atlas. Note: ibc – inside back cover

For the main index see pages 125–126

**Stevenson College Edinburgh
Bankhead Ave EDIN EH11 4DE**